**Dr. James L. Sullivan** is a native of Silver Creek in Lawrence County, Mississippi, where he first squinted at the light on March 12, 1910. The family then moved to Jackson, the capital, and finally settled at Tylertown in Walthall County, where James L. Sullivan graduated from high school.

He received the B.A. from Mississippi College, where he was captain of the football team which upset many of the football powers in the late twenties and early thirties. He then graduated (Th.M.) from Southern Baptist Theological Seminary, Louisville, Kentucky.

Before coming to the Sunday School Board he served the following churches: Boston, Kentucky (1932-1933); Beaver Dam, Kentucky (1933-1938); First Church, Ripley, Tennessee (1938-1940); First, Clinton, Mississippi (1940-1942); First, Brookhaven, Mississippi (1942-1946); Belmont Heights, Nashville (1946-1950); and First, Abilene, Texas (1950-1953).

He became executive secretary-treasurer (now president) of the Baptist Sunday School Board (Southern Baptist Convention) in 1953 where he has served for 22 years. Throughout his Board ministry Sullivan has traveled extensively, believing that a servant of Christ must stay with the people. He is the author of these previous books: *Your Life and Your Church, John's Witness to Jesus, Memos for Christian Living, Reach Out!,* and *Rope of Sand with Strength of Steel. God Is My Record* is his open, refreshing treatment of his convictions and reflections.

# Contents

# Foreword

This book makes no claims of perfection. Nor is it an effort to tell the full story of the past years in detail. To deal exhaustively with every facet would require multiple volumes. Rather, it is a cursory glance at the past, and a description of the part I had to play in it. It is in most abbreviated form. Too, it is written from a personal perspective. I describe things as I saw them. Others might have seen them differently from where they sat or stood.

By request I have given glimpses into my earlier years of life and training. Many have wondered how I have taken staggering problems relentlessly over such a span of years. Fortunately, God through my parents gave me an amazing body when it comes to endurance and resilience. Athletics stood me in good stead, too.

At the time of my first remembered physical examination, our old family physician said: "Son, if you don't live to be one hundred years old, it will be your own fault. I can't find a defect anywhere." But these years have demanded more than just a strong body. Even more important has been my philosophy, my attitudes. Never have I taken problems and criticisms personally. I have considered them inherent to the job, something that would come to any person holding the position I held. Thus, I never became morose or morbid.

The price I paid was the price leadership has to pay if it is to lead. No leader has ever escaped it. A man accepting major leadership responsibility and expecting only glory and roses will be disillusioned. He is apt to shatter mentally or physically or both.

These have been good years. True, I would not have worked as hard for anyone as I have for the Lord and Southern Baptists. I did it because I love and believe in both.

The title is a phrase I picked up from Paul as found in Philippians 1:8, which in its Scripture setting says, "For God is my record, how greatly I long after you all in the bowels of Jesus Christ."

Could I say more?

# 1
# Undeserved Blessings

God is good. He let me be born and bred at the buckle of the Bible Belt. The church was an integral part of our lives. Its people were our best friends. From earliest childhood we were taught to love books and "learning," to quest for knowledge, and to rejoice when we discovered a new truth. It was the Bible, however, that held a special place in our home and lives as the Book among books. We were taught to study its contents with devotion because it was a unique book given by God for a special purpose and would reveal truths we could never discover otherwise. We were taught to search for its deeper meanings, respect truth from heaven, and apply its teachings to our daily lives. The effect of such reverential treatment was profound. It played a vital role in the shaping of early attitudes, giving us bearings and a sense of values which are still firmly held in our lives.

While I could not argue that none of my attitudes have changed in the course of these years, I have to insist that those basic biblical beliefs are still the dearest I possess. With maturity and experience all of us take the teachings of others and make them our own through personal experience and application. By this process the meanings of Scripture passages oftentimes change, deepening in significance and importance.

How I came to a south Mississippi background runs far back in American history. The coming of my ancestors to the area dates almost from the time when that territory was nothing but a vastness of trees and swamps.

Mother's people, the Dampeers, entered Mississippi territory on a land grant signed by John Quincy Adams. Her people were Irish in background. They had heavy bodies and big bones. The body which

7

I received from them stood me in good stead during my athletic days. Being Celtic in background, the Irish are kin to the French. Mother's name had been spelled *Dampier* and was given a French pronunciation. French pronunciations, however, did not fit into the Mississippi spirit, so they anglicized it. Her people have been Dampeers ever since.

A Mississippi land grant was given in compensation for services rendered in the American Revolution. A settler still had to move across many miles to conquer the land from the Indians, clear it with his own hands, and hew out his own buildings for family occupancy. My ancestors seemed to thrive on such hard work in what is now Simpson County, Mississippi.

With the ending of the War Between the States, my grandfather returned home to get married and settle at Hebron in south central Mississippi. The nearest marketplace to grandfather was Wesson, Mississippi, on the Illinois Central Railroad. There he could sell or trade farm commodities for necessary supplies which he could not produce on his farm. One year after selling his crop he was waylaid by robbers while returning home in his ox wagon. Thus, he lost an entire year's work. The loss of such income brought increased hardship for several years before he recovered.

He made a habit of buying shoes for his large family of children by having each child stand on a piece of paper. With a pencil in hand he would outline the size and shape of their feet. This meant that shoes were approximately the right size, but never fit exactly, yet with growing feet this perhaps did not make much difference. For cloth he would buy a whole bolt at a time. Perhaps the best picture of the family group now in our possession is the one in which all the girls are wearing dresses made from the same kind and color of cloth. At least by such a method people could know to which family a child would belong at church or during some public event. Even that method had its advantages.

Later a railroad came through that area of the state and crossed my grandfather's farm, causing the country stores of Hebron to move across the hills to a site much nearer to grandfather's place. As a result, my grandfather ended up living only a couple of miles from town. He had not moved to town, but the town had moved to him! Mother was next to last in a large family of children. Her black, black hair and penetrating eyes made her most attractive. But her brain was what really distinguished her. Her mind worked almost like a modern-day computer. The slightest detail she could store away with ease, and her memory bank would call forth facts with accuracy and without strain. This made school not only easy for her, but a delight. She always excelled in scholarship, and one of her proud possessions was a solid gold, starshaped medal given her as a teenager. It bore the inscription "Mary Dampeer—Scholarship." It was no surprise that she made such an excellent teacher.

Mother's health was robust up to the time of my birth. I was the second birth, born fourteen months after my only brother, Arthur. I weighed twelve pounds at birth. With a head so large that buying hats has been a lifetime problem and with a large framed body, I could well understand how my birth left Mother with resultant health problems which she had to watch cautiously the rest of her years. She never complained, however, nor did she let this cause any of the children to be neglected in their needs or development. It merely meant that she lived with caution. Perhaps that worked to our advantage because she called on us to help her with chores, a fact that taught us to accept and discharge responsibilities from our earliest years.

My father's family came into Mississippi territory even before Mother's did. It is still one of the more famous—some would say infamous—families in the state. "Sullivan's Hollow" is as well known as any city in those parts, even though there is not one city of size within its boundaries. Only recently a movement spontaneously got under way to try to purchase the original Sullivan lands including the old family homeplace in which the eighth generation of Sullivans live. It should be done for historical purposes. A number of historic buildings are still standing nearby, including the log barns, smoke houses, and other facilities hewn from the virgin yellow pine timber so prevalent in early days when the territory was first being settled. The rolling lands are verdant, and if this movement succeeds, it will be preserving Mississippi history in living form. I have been made the keeper of a tool box about the size of a cedar chest with wooden hinges and dovetail corners in which tools were brought into Choctaw Indian territory and with which the earlier homes were hewn. Its age approximates that of our nation.

The Sullivan family, or clan, perhaps has been the most prolific in Mississippi history. There are more Sullivans and direct descendants of the Sullivans in the state than have issued from most any other family. The majority of them have stayed in the proximity of their birthplace and have remained unchanged in their life-styles.

Still, the unique trait about the Sullivans perhaps resulted from their intermarriages with relatives in their early days, much like the royal families of Europe. They married cousins. It was primarily because there were few other white women in the territory in those early days to whom they could offer proposals of marriage. Some of the boys married Indian girls, and some succeeded in finding Anglo girls in the area, but this intermarriage with cousins caused an imbreeding of family traits making family characteristics appear in exaggerated form—some glorious, others tragic. One of the best laughs I can remember came when I heard an old-line Sullivan telling a friend in all seriousness: "Sullivans of late have begun to marry among outsiders. In fact, they've married outsiders so often now that we've about reached that place where the Sullivans aren't any better than anybody else."

As the land was cleared and developed, it seemed that the ruffians either came in or emerged in great numbers, with the Sullivans sometimes adding to that number. As one friend put it, "What those Sullivans did, they did well." If they were gunsmiths, they were among the best. If they were bootleggers, the same principle held! They were not always careful about which profession they chose, but whatever it was they excelled in it.

The prevailing professions of the Sullivans aside from farming seem to have been teaching and preaching, much of the time simultaneously. Perhaps the greatest orator and most profound theologian of the lot was W. A. Sullivan, who for a quarter of a century pastored the First Baptist Church of Natchez, Mississippi. In college he had won the statewide oratorical contest and carried the same speaking skills to the pulpit with him as a pastor. His ability to deal with profound theological thought always fascinated me. It seemed so natural to him and served him well throughout his denominational life, even while he was president of the board of trustees of Mississippi College, his alma mater.

Several traits hold true almost universally about the Sullivans. Like the Iroquois Indians, they have no sense of fear. One frequently hears a saying in south Mississippi concerning them, "They will fight a buzz saw with a bear cat under each arm." Perhaps there's justification in such a saying because they will tackle anything fearlessly.

This fact nearly cost my father's life, if not my own. When I was sixteen years of age, a dangerous murderer from a family of killers was running loose in the country. Citizens were alarmed, even hysterical. They knew that somebody had to run great risk to capture him and bring him in. Dad, being of a fearless temperament, was deputized to do the job. He did. But that night a brother of the captured man, still running loose himself, came to our home with the avowed purpose of murdering my dad and criminally assaulting my mother as retaliation. Only later did we learn all the details, but that night we sensed something unusual about oddly shaping circumstances.

Dad happened to be away from home at that hour. Because it was a hot, humid Mississippi night, I had moved my cot into the hallway near the door leading to Mother's bedroom. No one could enter into her room without crossing my cot or my body. I was awakened by this murderous man trying to step over my cot. Without asking questions as to who he was or what he was doing there, I attacked him suddenly and furiously. He evidently was taken by such surprise that he fled into the darkness, and we never heard of him again.

Another trait of the Sullivans is rugged individualism. This is why nearly all are Baptists. Some of them are even of the more independent variety. So self-reliant are they as a breed that most any of them could be thrust into a forest alone. They would not only survive but would emerge safely with surplus game gathered in the interval. Being skilled outdoor people by nature, they are at home in the woods.

They love the hills, the trees, and the land, and are never lonely even when alone. Boredom seems to be unknown to them.

When my grandfather was just a boy, a "protracted meeting" (revival) was in progress, which drew saints and sinners alike. At times the sinners outnumbered the saints. Most of the persons present were Sullivans or kin to them. With a feud going on at the time, trouble was inevitable. Anyway, one gang met another gang on the churchyard, and hard fighting ensued. My grandfather heard the shots, climbed a tree, and watched the fight. Nine people were either killed or injured in the fray. One of the more robust ones was slashed with a razor-sharp knife across the abdomen. That slash laid open his middle. With his two arms he held himself in one piece and went over to the spring to wash his insides with spring water. He sent a friend to a nearby neighbor to borrow a needle and a spool of white thread, and proceeded to sew himself up! As unthinkable as it is in the days of modern-day surgery and bacteriology, he not only survived, but lived to die of old age!

Another relative was pastor of the church at this church meeting when the saints seemed to be in a minority. Determined that such utter lawlessness would not be permitted, he did not bother to call the law for protection. He simply armed himself with his own rifle and brought it to church with him. When the service began, he publicly laid it across the pulpit to keep order. System reigned from that time on. They used to tell it on this pastor that even while he prayed during those tense days he would lay the rifle across the pulpit and would pray with one eye shut and one open. When a curious friend asked him why, he got a terse explanation: "The Bible says, 'Watch and pray.' Given my circumstances I intend to do both—simultaneously."

With so many Sullivans, the mere matter of giving them names has been a problem. The prevailing names seem to be James, John, and Joe. Nearly every name has several Sullivans wearing it so they are forced to add other descriptive designations such as "Smokey Joe," "Tall James," "Short James," for the purpose of individualizing the person. Many times these nicknames describe a habit or a physical characteristic which become obvious to any observer, although this is not always the case.

The prevailing way of identifying an individual is by combining three generations of given names. My father was called Jim, and my grandfather's name was John Ben. It used to amuse me as a boy when I would go into Sullivan's Hollow. They would personalize me by calling me "Jimmy, Jim, John Ben." Of course, most everybody was a Sullivan.

Perhaps the one trait of the Sullivans which has stood us in as good stead as anything else is that inbred hatred of hypocrisy. Our insistence has always been that the absolute truth be told and faced whatever it is, whether good or bad. Nothing is more offensive to a Sullivan than trying to live in a world of make-believe and denying the hard realities that exist.

We were taught from the first to learn what the facts are, stay by the truth, "tell it like it is," and never try to dress up circumstances to make them mean something different from what they are. This psychology which has been drilled into us from the first has been advantageous in the ministry to which I have given my own life. Especially has this been true the last twenty-one years as I have served Southern Baptists as the chief executive officer of the Sunday School Board.

Even though I was born in Silver Creek, Mississippi, we have thought of Tylertown, a few miles south, as our home. My father had been in the contracting business with his brother Lon. The two of them had helped invent a hay baler which they were manufacturing in Silver Creek only a few miles from Mother's old homeplace when I was born. It was a typical deep South home with the porch, or veranda, completely circling the house except for one room at the rear. The home was near a clear, spring-fed branch with white sand called Silver Creek from which the town received its name.

Before I was two, my father had opportunity to go to Jackson, Mississippi, to help operate the Buckeye Cotton Seed Oil Mill there. While we were living in Jackson—I was three years old—our home burned in the wee hours of the morning. In fact, the first memory of my life came out of that vivid experience when my brother and I almost lost our lives in this raging inferno.

The light of the fire awakened a nearby neighbor. When he saw that the fire was in a room between our parents and our bedroom, he literally pulled us through the window, taking us under his arms to his own home. While he was rescuing us, he was calling for Mother and Dad. Evidently the noise did awaken them. They did not know that we had already been removed from the house. They were in despair when they saw the room in which we had been sleeping completely engulfed by flames. Only a few moments later they learned that we had been rescued without injury and were at a house next door.

Following the fire, Dad concluded that this would be a good time for him to make a move to another locality. He heard of a new town called Tylertown. The state had just authorized a new county and had made this small lumber and farming town its countyseat. Three railroads were under construction into the town from different directions to move the harvest of the huge pine timbers that literally covered the county except for the farmlands cleared by early settlers. The rest was open country and therefore excellent cattle country, providing us many cowboy experiences with horses and cattle on the open range.

One of the most fortunate aspects of the hometown was the strength of the institutions and the support the people gave them. The school was in a separate school district with one of the leading physicians of the community serving as chairman of the board. Leading citizens gave limitless time to building this institution of learning which far exceeded the quality of teaching for a town of that size in that day.

The church in large measure was the center of our lives and had a unique place, second only to the home. One of the first actions the local citizens took when the town first started was to build churches side by side so they could have a common graveyard nearby in which the earliest settlers could be buried. The two churches were the Baptist and the Methodist, which were virtually the same size. They were white wooden structures which could be identified as church buildings a great distance away. Each was one large room in which everything was conducted—teaching, worship, everything.

My first memory of the church was at Sunday School one morning after my brother and I had just gotten red patent leather shoes with black tops and tassles hanging on the side. I guess I must have been four years of age then. At teaching time the curtains were drawn around the various teaching groups. I found myself in the class with Mrs. Kate Ginn Ellzey, my first Sunday School teacher. Because my brother was a little older than I, he was in a class adjacent to mine. When I saw his red patent leather shoe with tassles sticking out from under the curtain separating the classes, I left my chair and went over to step hard on his toe. While I was gone, someone got my seat. So the first lesson of discipline I learned in the Sunday School grew out of the fact that my teacher would not require the boy who had gotten my seat to get up and return it to me. She said I had no business leaving it in the first place. One of my first lessons in Sunday School, therefore, did not deal with Bible content directly. Rather, it dealt with conduct in the house of the Lord, and I still remember it. That, too, was good "learning."

It was only a few years until the little one-room church building was wholly inadequate, so the members dedicated themselves to the erection of a new brick building which was the one I remember best. It was the place where I spent more hours than anywhere else in town except school and home.

Several memories about the Tylertown Baptist Church stand out. One is that it has had an array of outstanding pastors. Dr. W. A. Roper, grandfather of Dr. Lewis Nobles, present president of Mississippi College, was the pastor of my youth and the one with whom I had the closest associations. He was a scholar of the highest order, a Christian gentleman under every situation, and a man who perhaps understood the Bible and could preach the gospel as well as any pastor within the state. His scholarship was so excellent and his logic so deep that frequently as a child I would strain my brain to try to keep up with him, but I did. I reveled at his insights and interpretations. His sermons still have significant meanings to me.

Another thing about the church that I always appreciated was the outstanding leadership they provided for the youth of the church. It used to be the joke of the town that all beautiful girls came to Tylertown to teach and nearly all of them found husbands there. There was so much truth in this that it was more fact than joke.

Nearly all were Baptists because this was the predominant denomination in the area. These well-trained teachers became teachers and leaders in the church as well. They filled prominent roles because of their teaching skills.

So outstanding were my teachers that I can name them every one throughout my lifetime, and also can recall lasting contributions that each one made to my life. Perhaps the most skilled teacher I had in Sunday School was C. I. Brumfield. He was a professionally trained educator who had not only served as principal of the high school but during my years of youth was superintendent of education of the county. He was a "natural born" teacher. He not only knew how to communicate but how to make values that were really important stand out. His mode of teaching helped me to find my bearings and answer my natural questions while I was in my teenage years.

We never missed church. Still one of my most vivid memories was of our Saturday nights at home. The sights, sounds, and smells of Saturday night were different. I still recall the mixed odors of a cooking roast, Argo starch, and Shinola shoe polish. All were used simultaneously to prepare for the Lord's Day that followed.

Another contribution the church made to me was through the pastor himself. He was kind enough to let me use the books of his study when he was not using them. Too, he let me have the joy of distributing church literature secured from our denominational publishing house to all educational organizations. Perhaps he sensed from the first that I would read the various publications prior to distribution, which I did. Little did I dream during those years that the people whose writings I read with such interest and profit would become some of my best friends in subsequent years. Even less did I dream that I would ever be the executive head of that same publishing operation which served Baptist churches throughout the nation.

It still remains that the greatest influence of my life was the home in which I was reared. This is true not only because I spent more hours there than anywhere else, but because of the type of rearing my parents gave me. For my upbringing I am eternally grateful.

Mother was the spirit of the home. She always kept it at a high level of morale, teaching directly and indirectly in a manner that we were not aware of until later. Neither she nor Dad were ever overbearing in their disciplines or efforts to guide or dominate our lives. They were always clear in their expressed opinions. They let us know what they thought and where they stood, but most of our lives they left the decisions to us and simply told us what the consequences would be if we chose wrongly. In this they were fair. While there were a few times when the decisions were awfully difficult for us to make, I have come to believe this to be the best approach and have followed it with our own children.

Dad was a genius in motivating us as children to do what he thought was best for us without ever letting it become an issue. An illustration is when we were young boys. On a rainy day we wanted to build a lean-to, a rugged type of tent built out of heavily leafed limbs freshly cut. Mother felt we would catch our death of cold, so she was discouraging us the moment Dad came up. Without our knowing it he winked at her and said, "Let them go ahead." Actually, we had contended that we ought to be permitted to spend the night out and Mother knew that a night like that was not good for anyone's health.

Anyway, we hit for the woods with hatchets as quickly as we were given permission and almost worked our hands off getting the lean-to ready for our night out in the woods. Bedtime came all too quickly.

Dad had learned as a boy how a "whizzer" is made. It is a flat stick tied to the end of a string. When it is whirled, it makes a hair-raising, if not bloodcurdling, sound. Anyone who hears it and doesn't know what it is thinks it is some kind of wild animal lurking and threatening nearby.

When Dad thought it was time for us to come in and go to bed in our own beds, he took that whizzer which he had whittled for that special purpose. He sneaked to the opposite side of our lean-to from our home and whirled the whizzer five or six times. On the first whirl we straightened up. On the second whirl, my brother yelled, "Wildcat." With all haste we were safe and snug in our beds in a matter of moments. It was years later before we learned that it was Dad communicating that he thought time had come for us to go to bed. He knew we would argue if he called us, so he used his effective method. He did what was right without seeking to discipline directly.

My Father never told me I couldn't drink whiskey. He merely said: "Son, no parent can be with a child all of his life. If you want to drink, you will do it because I'm not with you all the time. You can get liquor at most any 'blind tiger joint' that you wish." But he continued: "The Sullivans are Scotch-Irish in background and have been heavy drinkers across the centuries. Alcoholism has been one of the major family problems." Because of that heritage the Sullivans are keyed up all the time 'in the key of gee-whiz.' If you smell one single stopper of hard liquor, you are apt to get dizzy, because your ancestors were drunk so many times over so many years all the way from Ireland. If I were you, I would leave it alone." That's all he ever said. I never had a desire to put a liquor bottle to my lips.

He used essentially the same approach with regard to smoking. Dad smoked occasionally himself and said to me: "If you want to smoke, that's your business, but I surely wish I had never started. I don't think it's good for a fellow, and especially if you're going to play athletics. I think you had better lay it aside, and it will be good for you and the game." As a result of that, I never touched a cigarette, either. This fact is what made it all the more amusing and amazing when as executive secretary of the Sunday School Board I was attending a city-wide meeting in Nashville when the evangelist was more negative than positive. In the course of his preaching, he was lambasting drinking, dancing, smoking, and many other practices. For some unexplained reason he threw in the statement, "It is a sin to smoke even if you are executive secretary of the Baptist Sunday School Board," then continued with his preaching.

The power of suggestion was illustrated when one of the women in the congregation came to me and spent two hours at my desk trying to convert me. She concluded I was not even a Christian. I not only smoked, she thought, but I was hypocritical and trying to hide it. Worse still, I wouldn't confess it. She was adamant in her condemnation of me because of what she thought was my secretiveness in the use of tobacco. The fact was that I had never had a cigarette in my mouth, but I could never convince her of it. She had assumed that when the evangelist threw this into his sermon, he must have known what he was talking about. Therefore, she felt called of the Lord to set me straight on the smoking issue.

I also have rejoiced in the psychological skills some other citizens of our town used in handling boys. One who lived near our home was Sam Grubbs who specialized in raising watermelons. He knew that stealing watermelons was always a temptation to growing boys, especially on hot summer days. So instead of waiting and dealing with us after we might have been tempted, he made the first approach. He came to us, explaining that he had a huge watermelon patch nearby. If we would help him look after it, he would give us one watermelon a day to take with us to the swimming hole. He kept his part of the agreement, and we kept ours. We were never tempted to take another one without his permission because we had been granted at least one a day with permission. The double value to him was that no one ever came in sight of his watermelon patch without every boy in the neighborhood climbing the fence yelling at the would-be thief. We proved to be the best protection Mr. Grubbs ever had for his ripening watermelons.

Dad also had an unusual avenue of working with us. I never remember his whipping me but one time and that was when *I made him do it*. As a four-year-old boy I had been climbing into the top of a huge hickory tree near our home. I even climbed up on the green shoots at the very top of the tree limbs which had not aged enough to support my young body. Mother had seen me up that tree several times and had suggested that I perhaps ought not to climb it. When Dad saw me there, he called me down and threatened, "The next time you climb that tree I'm going to give you a good brushing." He was employing a term his father had used in Sullivan's Hollow. While I did not know exactly what a brushing was, I found out the next day when I proceeded to do precisely what he had warned me not to do. I went to the top again, and he kept his word. It was the only whipping he ever gave me, but I have remembered it well.

On my first day of school, Dad called me in to have what he called a "man-to-man talk." He said: "Son, you go to school today. Let's have two understandings from the start. The first one is, I want you to know that the teacher is always right. Don't get into arguments with your teacher. If she tells me that you have been misbehaving, I'm going to take her word for it. And remember, if you get a whipping in school, you get another when you get home. I'm trusting you to tell me that you got one. Of course, I never got a whipping in school because I knew Dad meant what he said. I didn't argue, but Dad went on further to say: "If you will go all the way through school without failing, I will present you with the best watch that I can find at the time of your graduation."

When graduation came in high school, and I had succeeded in passing all my grades and was valedictorian of the class as well as class president, Dad said, "Now is the time for you to pick out the watch you want." I replied, "I've already picked it out." When he asked where it was, I said, "It's in your pocket. I want the watch that you got before you married." Dad, without saying a word, took it out of his pocket and gave it to me. I knew all the time that it was one of the most treasured personal possessions he had, but without hesitation he placed it in my hands because of a commitment that he had made the day I started to school.

One of my early memories was of a revival meeting in the old tabernacle of our town built for Gipsy Smith. It had its sawdust trail—literally. The benches were homemade. There were no external walls except behind the place where the preacher stood. Services were attended by multitides. While the singing was not of the highest in quality, it abounded in volume. I was still preschool in my years but two things about the service I recall. Both bordered on humor but in different ways. In the middle of the service, because there were no doors or walls, a toad-frog moved into the service in search of bugs falling from the kerosene lamps hanging from the ceilings. I was impressed that one would come to the services. I blurted out, "Look at that toader coming to church." My remark caused the people on our pew almost to fall off with laughter. The fact that the laughter had to be suppressed made it all the more painful.

I also recall that the preacher's sermon was on Jonah. He started by saying: "I'm preaching on a text tonight that a lot of people

disbelieve. I'm beginning with a question. I want a fast, honest answer.
Everybody here who honestly believes that Jonah swallowed the whale
lift his hand." Hands went up all over the place. The preacher chuck-
led, "I don't believe a word of it. I do believe that the whale swallowed
Jonah, but you'll never convince me that Jonah swallowed the whale."
His humor caught my attention as everyone laughed together. I
laughed, too, even though I didn't know the full meaning of it all
at the time. It was significant that after we arrived at home I asked
Mother to read the book of Jonah to me and tell me the story in
her own words. She did it and that book has been a precious book
to me ever since. It has more of the grace of God, missions, forgiveness,
the power of confession, and other cardinal doctrines than any other
Old Testament writing. This was my introduction to it.

As a boy, I enrolled in Sunbeams. Miss Belle Rimes who was my
leader is still alive. Here I received my first concept of modern-day
mission work.

One of the pinnacles of my life came when one of our neighbors
who was director of BYPU (Baptist Young People's Union) walked
out in his front yard with a little girl one and one half years old.
She was holding his finger. He was Homer Scott, local druggest, who
was keeping the child for his brother Ernest whose wife had just
died.

I went home to tell my Mother that there was the prettiest little
girl I had ever seen up at Mr. Scott's house. I didn't know then who
she was, but I liked the way she looked. It turned out that this beautiful
young girl who impressed me so at first sight still does. She is my
wife and the mother of my three children. In fact, she has been an
indispensable helpmeet to me through my years in the gospel ministry.
She is the only girl I ever dated, and the only girl with whom I
have ever been in love. I counted that meeting one of the most
fortunate days of my life when I met her at a time she was too young
to have an opinion about me. She and I never had but five formal
dates. The fifth one was the wedding date. We've known each other
almost as long as our memories run back and have found our lives
to be most compatible in the things we're interested in, the objectives
we're trying to accomplish, and the love we share. Of course, our

coming from a comparable background has also been helpful in our marriage and has contributed to the happiness of our home.

Through the years, I have mulled over the way my brother and I interrelated our lives. Actually, we intertwined them so that we operated more like twins than merely brothers. We looked very much alike and were often mistaken for twins, but we weren't. We did function almost as twins. While we were inseparable, our approaches and modes of operation were different, but each undergirded the other in his decision-making process and in his actions.

My brother was the daring type. He was extremely creative, willing to undertake almost anything once. With a fertile mind he was always finding ways to be inventive. His mode of operation was not too different from John Foster Dulles, past secretary of state, whose life was a living illustration of "brinkmanship."

I was the other type person who was always analyzing each situation. I would criticize his deeds, telling him how he could do a better job next time. I was observing his actions objectively. I operated more like a philosopher or judge. He was more of an activist. It is interesting that when he became a lawyer and I became a preacher that he surrounded himself with men like me, and I surrounded myself with men like him. The life-styles we developed in childhood became lifetime models for us.

# 2
# Unforgettable People and Lessons

On several occasions people have asked where I find my illustrations. They often ask what kind of filing system I use in calling illustrations into focus when needed in sermons and messages. Actually, I have no planned system at all. Instead, my problem is to keep from using illustrations too frequently. Many times I find myself having to sort some out even while the message is in progress.

Why this is I cannot say. Temperament and training have much to do with this. I have always been a close observer and have tried to analyze things in detail while they were happening. The power of recall has been easy, so illustrations are prevalent in my messages. Dr. W. O. Carver once asked me how I handled my illustrations in preaching after I had brought a series of messages on Ephesians at Ridgecrest. He commented, "I never had any problem with scholarship, but I did with illustrations." He said, "I wish that I had learned to use illustrations as a young man, but I have never felt at ease putting them in my messages." My own experience has been exactly the opposite.

Evidently, I learned in early years to think in concepts, pictures, and analogies. I find myself somewhat like James, the writer of the New Testament book by that name, who in a dozen verses in the first chapter calls up perhaps a dozen analogies in order to convey diverse concepts about Christian living. I think I got many of my thought patterns and modes of expression from the black "mammies" with whom we associated daily in childhood years in an era now gone forever. Their influence holds. They thought and taught us to think in pictures and concepts, learning much of this from their preachers who were mighty in the pulpit and colorful in expressions.

Many of my illustrations emerge from my own experiences—perhaps the majority of them from out of my athletic years. Admittedly, my athletic experiences were unique because I played football long before it became a prominent sport in our part of the country. There was much imagination and creativity added to the game as we tried to figure how we were to deal with certain situations when we were trying to play football even before we had a rulebook or even a ball.

One of my early memories of football was when the boys in our family challenged the boys of a neighboring home to a game near our house—in a lane lined by a barbed wire fence. While this created a hazard of a sort, it also solved some problems for us. We didn't know what you were supposed to do when you ran out of bounds anyway. To make matters worse, we had pooled our money but could not find a store in town with a football for sale. We ended up playing with a molasses bucket. We were faced immediately with the problem of starting the game. As one of the boys remarked, "You can't start off the game by kicking the bucket." We decided to start with a toss. The other boys won the toss so they had the first chance with the ball. They made a good run on the first play. On the second run one of their players was put to bed because of injury. It was not that he was tackled too hard. He fell on the "ball."

It was a couple of years from that time that thirteen of us decided we would try to get football going in the high school. We faced many problems. In the first place, there was no budget provided for athletics. Whatever budget there may have been was put into the employment of a woman athletic director of mass calisthenics for the entire study body. She doubled as teacher of dramatics and expression in the school. It was natural that we would turn to her when we decided to go ahead and build a team when the trustees told us they had no objection. This brave lady agreed to direct a minstrel show for the purpose of raising money. Then we would by public subscription obtain a freewill offering from the citizens of the town who gathered to see the minstrel.

The idea worked. We were able to collect enough money to buy uniforms for thirteen boys, even though we had barely enough for eleven pairs of shoes. This meant we had to change shoes every time we sent in a substitute, but there was not much substituting then, anway. We had only two surplus players in the beginning.

Since we had only enough money to buy our outfits without money enough to hire a coach, we asked the woman who was in charge of mass calisthenics, Miss Gladys Kirkwood, if she would coach the team. To our surprise she accepted. So we were one of the first football teams of the nation to have a woman coach and a successful one at that! Fortunately, she had been a cheerleader in college and had observed the science of the game. She was able therefore to help us learn the principles of blocking, tackling, and punting. This laid good groundwork for our first season of play.

After the town saw that we meant business, some of the leading citizens got their heads and pocketbooks together to employ a man coach to finish out the season. Mr. Walter Simmons who had played in college and was operating a farm nearby drove in each afternoon to direct us. In those experiences we learned how to work together as a team or we never would win. We learned how to solicit the support of the community behind a common project. We learned the value of discipline in order to develop strong bodies. We learned how to be creative in the solving of problems that we had never faced before.

I was fortunate during those days because I was really not old enough to play on a high school team. I was only thirteen and in the eighth grade. But there were no limitations about age or classification to be eligible for the team. Anyone made it if he could, and didn't if he couldn't. Even when I was that age, I weighed more than 150 pounds so I began playing as an eighth grader and played every game until graduation. In fact I played most of every game until I finished high school five years later because the idea of platoons had not caught on.

These were delightful years that kept us out of mischief and gave us real opportunities to work together on a project in which we were mutually interested. I rejoiced in the opportunity. I had the privilege of serving as captain of the team during both my junior and senior years. This brought additional learning experiences that would not have been mine otherwise.

It was in Mississippi College, however, where the game really became a fascinating experience. I played all four years in college, giving me nine years of football experience. Too, I had the joy of being captain at Mississippi College my senior year under Coach Stanley Robinson who was perhaps as outstanding as any small college coach of the nation. He was recognized as such by his peers.

Coach Robinson graduated from Colgate University in New York after having been reared in Buffalo in that state. He first came South to coach at Mississippi State University. Later he came in contact with little Mississippi College which had a player by the name of "Goat" Hale. Together they defeated every team they played regardless of size. So outstanding was this player that when Tulane University was defeated 13 to 0, the paper in New Orleans had a big headline across the top: *"Goat" Hale 13—Tulane 0.* His record still stands as one of the nation's best.

Coach Robinson had a profound influence on my life because of the quality of man that he was. He was a fanatic for clean play. He participated for the sheer sport of playing; his attitudes influenced my own.

Coach did not like giving scholarships to athletes. He wanted a player to play because of his love for the game and not because he was getting a supplementary income for doing so. Coach abhorred anyone who was unfair in competition. While he trained us to play hard, we learned right off that he would jerk a man from the game as quickly for playing unfairly as for anything else. He never allowed foul language on the gridiron. He taught us well how to block and tackle and how to carry out the fundamentals of the game. He gave us a superb example in the quality of living he expected us to follow.

Coach Robinson kept himself in excellent physical condition and could vie with any of us in physical combat. I can see him now with cap in hand running behind a slow runner tapping the boy on his helmet with that cap. He would yell to the top of his voice: "Run, run. You could cross a basket of eggs and never crack a shell."

Coach scheduled games for us at distant places to give us opportunity for broad travels. We played the University of Mexico in Mexico City. Two weeks later we played Colgate University in Hamilton, New York, coach's alma mater. This was before the days of airplanes so we traveled in a special railroad car leased for that purpose.

During the football season, we spent endless hours going to distant places, but we learned valuable lessons in doing so. Between the game with the University of Mexico and Colgate, we had a practice game in Soldiers' Field in Chicago. It was in a blizzard which was painful because we hadn't yet seen a frost in the deep South. Bo McMillan's team was en route to New York to play there over the weekend. We had a scrimmage game with them in Chicago.

The same blizzard held as we played Colgate University in New York later. We had never seen football players play with mittens. Coach laughingly told it that on the first play we had the ball and Colgate had eleven pairs of mittens. On the second play they had the ball and we had the eleven pairs of mittens! We had snatched them from their hands during play. It wasn't quite that universal, but one of the boys actually did do so because the extreme cold hurt his hands so badly.

Perhaps the most memorable game of my nine years of football was with Mississippi State University at their homecoming. It was one of the most closely fought games of my football experience. It ended with our defeating them 4 to 3. That is an odd score, but it illustrates how hard we fought to win. It was the only time I was ever so exhausted physically when the final whistle blew that I couldn't walk to the dressing room until I had taken time to rest.

In the final moments of the game, Mississippi State had brought the ball to our one-yard line. We held them four consecutive plays to get possession of the ball and punt out. The unbelievable thing was that the safety man caught the ball and ran back to our one-yard line. This means we had to hold them four more consecutive times. I was in the linebacker position on defense. This means that we had to hold them eight consecutive times on defense within the one-yard line! We did so and the final whistle blew before we got opportunity to punt the ball out of the end zone. Nevertheless, we won the game. Of course, there was great rejoicing because ours was a small college playing one of much larger size with bigger men. So much for athletics.

Concerning my own conversion and Christian experience, it is hard to say just which person influenced me the most or caused me to think most seriously. Many helped. I always felt that I had the best teacher in the Sunday School as well as the best teacher in the school. I worked hard in preparation for every teacher. I enjoyed them all.

My conversion experience was a memorable one. I remember the day well. Fortunately, I can pinpoint the place as well, and can recall vividly the depth of my own emotional commitment. The encounter I had with Christ that day has had a lasting influence on all my attitudes and actions.

Our pastor was bringing his regular Sunday morning message. While all of his sermons were outstanding, this one seemed to be pinpointed to meet my own needs and answer some problems with which I had been personally wrestling. Previous experiences had not yet brought me to that point of definite decision.

When the sermon was over I went directly home. I know now that Mother understood fully what my problem was because of the way she talked with me when I told her I wasn't hungry and didn't care for dinner. Rather, I asked if I could get my favorite horse and go horseback riding. She readily agreed. Evidently she knew I was wrestling with some personal matters, and she wanted me to be alone so that I could work through my own decisions in my own way. I appreciated her feeling of freedom to let me make up my own mind.

I went to what we called "Lover's Mountain." It is perhaps the highest point in the county, a beautiful place in nature just above Magee's Creek, where we spent so many of our youthful years fishing, hunting, and swimming. I tied my horse to a nearby tree and spent literal hours in meditation and prayer trying to come to that point of a personal decision on my own. The day was drawing to a close. Still I felt that I had not received the answer for which I was questing. If I were to go back to BYPU and church that evening, however, I had to be on my way. So I mounted the horse and was riding home alone. I had gotten in sight of the church when I actually experienced a change of mind, heart, attitude, and feeling. Burden was turned to joy. Doubts were removed by a vibrant faith which has continued with me throughout my years. Of course, I went on to church that evening, made my newfound faith publicly known and was received as a candidate for church membership.

While I was unable to understand all the ramifications of what occurred in that youthful moment, I knew that God was doing something wonderful in my heart which would be a lasting influence in my life. As I look back across the years on it, I'm convinced that God was impressing me also at that moment that he wanted me in the gospel ministry. I began to feel immediately that my life should be cast in that direction although it was years later before I ever told anyone even in confidence or made a formal announcement to that effect.

In fact, I was seventeen years of age before I made my earlier impressions known. Instead of it being an announcement, it was simply an admission even then in a classroom where we were talking about various professions open to us as young people. It was then that one of my dearest friends said: "Everybody knows that you're going to be a preacher. Why don't you just go ahead and announce it?" I did forthwith in that same civics class of which Miss Hazel Ruff was the teacher. The thing that amazed me most was the interest and support I got from the entire class which was closely knit. The class still holds reunions every five years. They were the type classmates who pulled the best out of each other.

Hard times followed my high school years. It is a miracle that I ever got through college and I would not have succeeded had not many people given me strategic opportunities at crucial times. Miss Addie Mae Stevens was one of these, secretary to Dr. J. W. Provine, president of the college. She asked me if I'd like to work a few hours each day posting grades and doing routine office tasks. Not only did this income enable me to continue my education without interruption but on the job I found Miss Addie Mae a superb teacher of sound management practices. Her instructions were not only remembered, they have been practiced throughout my years at the Sunday School Board. Many other students were not so fortunate.

To name people who have had a profound influence in my life would demand that I call attention to a special contribution made by Dr. W. H. Sumrall. He was one of my major professors during college years, first in the field of history and then in psychology. Even though he had meant much to me as a teacher and I appreciated his instructions tremendously, it was after college that he made his major contribution to me and my preaching. I had requested an interview with him and tried to evaluate my pulpit ministry as pastor of the church at Clinton, Mississippi. The church was adjacent to the college and the majority of the members were either students or faculty members. It was a tremendous place for a rewarding pastorate.

Even though I worked and studied hard in sermon preparation, I felt that my preaching was not accomplishing what I felt it should. I had gone to Dr. Sumrall with a simple question, "What kind of preaching really ministers to your heart and life?" He thought a moment while he fingered my lapel. He then said: "I like philosophy and psychology. I have majored in these and even teach in these fields so I am committed to their influence and worth. At the same time, when I come to church I want pot liquor and cornbread. I want simple preaching, straight from the shoulder, straight to the heart." This comment revolutionized my preaching more than any course I ever took in homiletics. I had been paying more attention to scholarship and content than to communication. Dr. Sumrall led me to see that regardless of the level of one's educational achievements when he sits as a worshiper in a congregation he wants to be a simple worshiper, humble and searching before God.

From that moment to this I never preached a sermon that could not be understood by any "Junior" boy or girl in the congregation. As surprising as it might be, it takes twice as much preparation to preach a simple sermon as it does a complex one. A preacher is trained to think in terms of theology, so he does his sermon preparation in the light of that training and background. The process of simplification at that point is almost like a translation as the message is put into the language of the man of the streets. This sort of an approach, however, enables one to be profound in content and simple in expression. I have tried to make this the style of my preaching.

# 3
# What I Came to Do

Leaving the pastorate was a painful experience for me because I loved everything about my years of close relationship to local congregations. The churches I served were different but they were all interesting. I loved the people. I sought to meet their spiritual needs both in messages and personal visitation. Too, we tried to develop programs that would help them grow and mature to their highest potential.

The routine I followed throughout those pastoral years was similar, although the churches varied in size from small to large. I usually averaged speaking once a day. Therefore many hours had to be spent in preparation of messages of various kinds to keep abreast with the times and to make messages applicable to the situation. During those years one of our small children was asked, "What does your daddy do?" She shot back her unhesitating reply, "He just studies all the time." Her statement had a great deal of truth in it because daily messages do require intensive and constant study.

I used Mondays to visit the people who had joined the church the day before. Tuesday and Thursday were my hospital days; Wednesday was my day of visiting uptown, making contacts with the business and professional people of the community. Friday was the day in which I concentrated on prospects for church membership. Saturday was a light day in the schedule. I usually gave it to the family because the children were out of school on that day. This was the time for our family outings and relaxation from the relentless pressures of the pastorate. Each day as opportunity came I would talk to non-Christians of the community about their spiritual needs and try to direct them to a personal relationship in Christ. Of course, interspersed across all those days were multitudinous committee meetings and planning sessions to keep the vast and complex educational organizations of the church moving.

I gave one hour immediately after lunch each afternoon to inter-
views in the church office with people who had personal needs or
who wanted to talk with the preacher about something on their hearts
and minds.

Another routine I followed rather systematically was that of accepting one revival meeting *each quarter* of the year. I followed this course
most of my pastoral ministry. I would be in a country church, a college
town, a countyseat church and a city church once each year. Such
a course gave me diversified experiences and opportunities as I
preached in four revivals annually.

While I had not planned it that way, my pastoral experience on
both sides of the Mississippi River and in the deep South, as well
as in Kentucky and Tennessee, gave me geographical coverage that
was unique. This enabled me to maintain a grasp of the different
types of situations existing in Southern Baptist life. It was profitable
to me later when I entered more into denominational affairs to learn
that while Baptists are similar in basic biblical beliefs, they have very
different attitudes, concepts, vocabulary, and speed of operation. A
denominational worker must come to understand this fact either
through instruction or experience. Otherwise he's apt to create more
problems than he solves.

The First Baptist Church at Abilene was one of the happiest situations in which I could ever be engaged as a pastor. It was a strategic
distribution center of West Texas. Many outstanding citizens were
Baptists. The church was at the very heart of the community in an
influential and profound way.

Dr. T. L. Holcomb had served for eighteen years as executive
secretary-treasurer of the Sunday School Board and was coming to
retirement. Maxey Jarman, president of General Shoe Corporation,
was named chairman of the special committee of trustees to recommend a successor. He called me to explain that the committee had
come to feel that I ought to accept this responsibility. While I appreciated the committee's confidence, because I knew the quality of men
serving on the committee, I was reluctant. I remember that I was
also called by W. A. Criswell who served as a member of the nominat-

ing committee. He encouraged me to give serious consideration to the request.

It was difficult for me to reach the place of answering yes to the committee. In fact, I came to Nashville for a conference first to discuss in depth with the committee some of the things that I needed to know before I could seriously consider its offer. Matters were complicated all the more because we were in the midst of a million dollar building project in Abilene where I had been pastor less than three years. Nevertheless, I was not able to remove this matter from my heart and mind until I agreed to accept and allowed my name to be presented for the responsibility.

Having served on the Sunday School Board as trustee for four of the years that I was pastor in Nashville at Belmont Heights Baptist Church, I knew something of the complexity of the operation. I understood the intense responsibilities internally and externally, and changes which were inevitable if the work load were to be distributed. The financial load that one had to carry and the balance one had to maintain under every conceivable pressure would be difficult. From a close position I had watched Dr. Holcomb bear up under the load when at times it seemed impossible for any one man to handle so many things. I had wondered how a person's health could survive for long when such demands would never let up. Nevertheless, I could not bring myself to the place of saying no to the trustees even though personally I knew it would be a sacrifice to my family as well as to myself. I knew, too, that it would reduce the number of hours I could spend with my children. They had to be involved in the process of decision making, too.

When everything was cleared and the committee was given a green light, the Board proceeded to vote on the matter. The invitation was extended me officially and the date for my assumption of responsibility was set for June 1, 1953.

My own disposition had led me to conclude that the first year in office ought to be spent largely in study and evaluation. I felt major decisions could best be made the second year, then people would not misunderstand my actions. They would not feel then that I was reflecting on my predecessor by changes I was making in the operation. It would not look like I was competing with his record. In the pastorate I had followed this procedure. Through each first year I had met the people, analyzed the situation, penciled in my concepts of where the church ought to go and how. Then the second year we would launch into an aggressive program of advance. I would be competing with my own record of achievement then and all would be well.

I found that the situation in Nashville would not allow the luxury of delay. I found myself having to make major decisions almost by the time I arrived in town. Dr. Holcomb was frank to say to me that he felt a reorganization of the Board was necessary and ought to be done as quickly as humanly possible. He pointed out that it had been needed for sometime but his age could not stand the strains of such major changes as were required. I found that he was right. I had to move immediately into that course.

On top of major administration decisions, many things were required of me by the Board bylaws such as initialing vouchers and signing checks, interviewing personnel, and approving individual actions of employees. Still I had to find time enough to develop and recommend a better way of relating and utilizing both trustees and employees for maximum efficiency in an on-going operation that was expanding rapidly.

This meant many nights without sleep except for catnaps because the reorganization details had to be worked out after the day's work was done. After the system was developed, new employees had to be chosen for each position, new procedures had to be established and training had to be done. Then the major transition had to be done simultaneously so that everything would fit together and move in a new direction the moment changes were effective. The fact that everything was dated only complicated this already complex experience of transition.

I accepted the offer of the Board to be the executive secretary-treasurer of the institution because I had in mind and heart a number of things I felt ought to be done. I could engage in these activities with personal conviction because I felt that they were compatible with the outlook and direction of my life. I could be happy in that type of situation.

Some of the objectives immediately before us were: (1) to push for a numerical growth in the educational organizations in the churches especially in Sunday School, Church Training, and Church Music; (2) to correlate the programs and activities of church organizations to which we would be related so that they could work in harmony with each other and toward common goals previously established and agreed to; (3) to relate all program organizations to the local church itself in such a way that they would see themselves as an integral part of the church's life existing to carry out the church's wishes; (4) to produce the best type of religious education materials available to any denomination with attractive illustrations, sound curriculum and good communication; (5) to provide diversity both in education and publications so that we could meet the needs of every type of church in every conceivable situation in Southern Baptist life; (6) to bring to the Board the most capable people we could find in their areas of respective assignment, people committed to the high spiritual purposes of the institution and the objectives of the Convention itself; (7) to establish an in-training program which would help each person understand his job better and do it with skill. Our objective was for each person to accomplish more with less effort; (8) to provide facilities in which our employees would work which would reflect our high concept of their worth as persons and the importance of the job they were doing, to provide these necessary buildings without creating undue indebtedness against the institution; (9) to provide salaries for the workers which were commensurate with the salaries of people in comparable positions elsewhere, especially those agencies and institutions from which most of our personnel would come; (10) to provide internal operations which would keep our employees healthy and in good mental attitudes toward their work with professional counsel being provided to help them in their personal lives so that problems could be solved in the quickest and easiest ways; (11) to consolidate operations within the Board that were similar so that the same thing would not have to be done in several different departments. We felt the work could be done in one place and have information shared with others in an efficient and effective manner; (12) to increase our efforts in public relations, seeking to interpret the institution to the community in which we were located and seeking also to communicate its actions, activities, and available programs and to interpret our purposes to the public the nation over; and (13) to operate as economically as we could by increasing productivity, synchronizing the efforts of workers as we could find better technical processes for doing a good job at lesser cost.

These were some of the major objectives I had in mind upon coming to the Board. While I did not establish consecutive priorities concerning the implementation of each, I have sought to keep each in mind during the course of my entire tenure. My philosophy called for reaching toward these objects while remaining true to the Bible, warm in spirit, and forward in outlook. I saw opportunities of advance in all these areas. I pushed for these objectives before the appropriate committees of the board of trustees to get them approved and to get movements of advance underway.

Some of the objectives were not as formally developed and stated as others, but all have been existent throughout the entire tenure. After getting underway, circumstances arose which sometimes caused delayed implementation or shifts in timetable.

Personally, I have never been the pushy type. I have never sought to bulldoze a program through when it did not have the support of the workers or constituency. My own temperament has called for me to make proposals concerning what I thought was best, dealing with every conceivable detail in preparation and implementation. If opposition arose during the implementation, and it usually did, I would seek to throttle down or adjust activities so that the enemies could become friends and the movement continue toward its goal. People who opposed the project often would see that they were wrong in their suppositions. I would give them opportunity to shift positions and become cooperative in the endeavor rather than for us to shove the program through regardless of the attitudes of the people either inside the Board or in the Convention.

While such a strategy has not always worked smoothly, it has stood us in good stead. It has elicited a firmer support on the part of workers for the denomination as well as the members of local churches throughout the country. Of course, we could never wait until everything was unanimous because nothing could ever be done that way. Experience has shown that approximately 20 percent of the people will either be indifferent or tend to oppose any program or activity even though you have done your utmost to involve everyone in the planning process and have done your dedicated best in communication with all. This should not be surprising, however, when we analyze human nature and the way people think.

Merchants throughout the world know that no retailer can sell to more than 80 percent of the people. Not everyone will buy from the same firm. Even Sears and Roebuck can't sell to everybody. For some reason, research shows that merchants can sell to about 80 percent of the constituency of a community, but 20 percent will resist or refuse to purchase anything from them regardless of price or quality of the commodity offered.

It may be shocking to the average pastor to realize that approximately 20 percent of the congregation to which he may go as pastor are apt to be against him the day he arrives in town—sight unseen, before he has met one of them and before they know the type of man he is. But because he is pastoring human beings, this is a response he might as well expect. It is an inevitable experience to every person in leadership whether he's in politics, business, or religion. This human equation holds. A leader had better be aware of it and learn to adjust to it.

While I came to the Board to perform certain definite tasks and felt that I would be able to launch into them full scale immediately, I found a different world emerging only a matter of months after my arrival. I came in June, 1953. With the noted 1954 Supreme Court decision on public school racial segregation the following year, everything the nation over was thrown into social upheaval. As new laws were rewritten within that interpretation, human patterns were adjusted and new legal requirements were made. Businesses had to operate on different principles, federal laws and regulations became multitudinous and oftentimes contradictory, decisions of various bureaucratic sections of government became conflicting, and all institutions involved in interstate commerce were seeking answers. Seldom was there consistency in the replies and responses received from the government. So administration became increasingly difficult each passing year.

We did see tremendous increases in Sunday School enrollment as well as in Church Training and baptisms because of the increased number of people reached for Bible study. Even now many people look back on the "Million More in '54" effort as one of the finest periods of advances the denomination has known. Every area had healthy growth. Almost fantastic support and participation were given by the people.

Soon the situation began to change the psychology of the nation, however, and this began to take its toll on the attitudes of the people generally. Society began to enter complex eras of transition. Revision and change tended to bring emotional exhaustion to the people and made them feel deeply that they were being manipulated, even though they were not always aware of causes and effects. Still they reacted strongly and acted like they were shell-shocked. Communities were torn asunder by arguments on social issues about which recent federal laws had been written and court decisions rendered. Most affected by these complex and often baffling federal regulations were the geographical areas where Southern Baptist strength was greatest.

The strategy the Sunday School Board should follow had to be developed. Processes had to emerge. Steps taken had to be sound, never compromising, New Testament principles. New vocabularies had to be developed. Meanings of the words had to be translated to the people almost en masse. Words that had once possessed certain meanings came to have entirely different, if not opposite, meanings. Communication became more complex. Never with all these changes did the Board alter its objectives, but we found ourselves many times having to alter timetables.

As I implied earlier, the social upheavals, the changes in public psychology, plus efforts to streamline the organization within the Southern Baptist Convention under the Branch Committee, brought pressure on everyone. Then within the numerous state conventions and with a new grading system and new modes of operations as well as new titles of educational positions in local churches, time was required for readjustment.

As we were beginning to emerge with some degree of normalcy out of these necessary organizational changes we thought had to be made, the rebellious sixties were on us. We found ourselves head on with situations quite different from anything ever anticipated. Every institution of size and influence came under attack simply because it was there. Opposition forces became more numerous. Newspaper attacks seemingly became more popular against colleges, businesses, certain professions, and religious organizations and institutions such as ours. Nor did local churches escape. It would be an interesting study for a professional analyst to find out why this was true. All persons with responsibilities felt the painful difficulties we were inevitably facing in situations that we had not anticipated. Administration of any kind became more difficult and complex.

Perhaps the major change was in the physical expansion program of the Board. Unexpected opportunities developed here that made it possible for us to purchase land the Board had sought to acquire for decades. We had acute need for expanded facilities in which our people could do their necessary work more comfortably. We did not want any of our workers to labor in low-grade buildings or sweatshop situations. While the purchase of new property and the erection of buildings were tremendously expensive, we have been able to build some of the best quality buildings in Nashville. They have all been paid for, with no remaining debts for future budgets to care for. Such massive building projects were not on a priority list, but because the situation became opportune, we moved that way with full speed. The same expansion concepts were implemented in book store operations and in the two assemblies—now called conference centers—at Ridgecrest and Glorieta.

Previously, we had tried to do literature shipping in the basement of the lower building. There was only one loading dock on one side of the building through which materials could be brought. Another loading dock was on the other side where the filled mail sacks were loaded and carried to the post office. This was not only physically hard, but at times the handling of such volume through such small corridors approached impossibility. Trucks with printed materials would sometimes wait two and three hours merely to reach the loading dock. After the mail had been sorted and placed in mail bags, each sack had to be lifted manually and placed over a conveyer chain after it had been weighed. It was loaded on a truck by hand, taken to the post office, and manually unloaded. With hundreds of tons of materials each year having to go through this difficult process, it is understandable that we would reach that point of sheer mathematical impossibility where such volume could no longer be handled in such an awkward manner.

It was providential that more than five acres of downtown property became available to us. It had been formerly a freight house jointly owned by the L and N and NC and St. L railroads. With such acreage we could put everything on two floors, spread out the floor space between Broadway and Church streets and not have to use elevators for constant up and down movements in shipment.

Previously, an electric cart was used in the shipment of literature. It would go to a hoist to be lifted to another level. It would cross through the basement of the entire building to another elevator only to go up several floors to load materials. Then it would reverse the process simply to convey the materials to a shipping point. Knowing that every handling of materials is expensive as well as time consuming, we had to do something. Now all the orders can come in one end of the building, are classified and sorted according to subject matter, and are processed through a systematic classification and distribution system. With modern techniques and instruments, the zip coded mail bags are made ready for distribution. These are attached to an underground conveyer chain taking them directly to the post office, past the post office directly to a distribution center, so nothing has to be handled by hand now. Very little has to be trucked except that for local distribution.

All of the literature now is handled on the first floor in the Operations Building which is almost one fourth of a mile in length. Five football fields can be placed on the roof. Book stores supplies are handled on the floor above in the same general system of operation which has been developed so that the flow of the materials is almost endless. All is done with a minimum of effort and time.

While we have had massive expansion and building programs in the city of Nashville of necessity to handle the enlarging operations, it has been fortunate and providential that we have been able to secure the land we needed for years to come. We have erected the buildings that seem to be needed for the immediate future in Nashville. Some of the land we've had to buy on a square-foot basis at prices seeming exorbitant. Without exception, however, the value of these properties has increased after the purchase. Experience has shown that all have been economical in the light of what has been saved by providing adequate facilities for the work to be done.

We have built a number of Baptist Book Stores. The Board has a rather long-range plan whereby the trustees authorize a building after a study shows that it is best for us to own a building in a certain city. Parking must also be provided for those who come to make the purchases of the church materials needed. Historically, the Sunday School Board has sought to locate Baptist Book Stores in buildings where the state convention offices have been located. This was feasible when most of these buildings were at the heart of the cities. Appropriate sales floors could be provided and usually there was heavy foot traffic on the sidewalks out front. With the unfolding of time, however, many of these state convention offices have moved to the suburbs where retail operations are most difficult. This has forced us to relocate a number of stores, or to add supplementary stores in a city where such would be more readily accessible to buyers and convenient for church members.

Some of the most expensive building additions to be erected were at Ridgecrest and Glorieta to meet the requests of our constituency and to provide the type of facilities needed for the various conferences. Not only have we had to build Glorieta from the ground up, but we also had to update the facilities at Ridgecrest. Because of age and inadequacy, many of the old wooden buildings put up in the earliest days of that assembly had seen their days of usefulness.

Of course, Dr. Holcomb was executive secretary when the Convention voted that Glorieta be the location of the Western Assembly. He led in the long-range planning using the Church Architecture Department to work out many of the details. General layouts were developed to show possible locations of buildings, the necessary roads, power lines, water and sewer facilities and other considerations that would be necessary to its existence. Approximately one and one half million dollars had to be spent before a brick could be laid on the grounds. Roads had to be constructed and utilities provided before building could get under way. Dr. Holcomb was able to see the roads graded and surfaced. He also saw the completion of the front part of New Mexico Hall, the first unit of the dining hall, the chapel part of the Holcomb Auditorium, the old Texas Hall, later destroyed by fire, and the middle sections of Oklahoma Hall, as well as the Hall of States, Spruce Lodge, and Pine Lodge.

It was at that point that I came on the scene as his successor. This means it has been my responsibility to add two new wings to New Mexico Hall, two additional units to the dining hall, the wings of the existing dormitories, the Children's Building, the larger auditorium and a host of other buildings supportive and supplementary to an operation. Actually a city within itself has been built where all facilities had to be provided for us for use, even the fire department and safety devices required by law. Of course, all of us wanted safety for all of the people attending the conference centers.

At Ridgecrest, we've had to replace Spilman Auditorium, Pritchell Hall, and Rhododendron, as well as quite a number of additional new buildings for education and housing. There are still some more dormitories and apartments necessary to upgrade Ridgecrest to the level we think it ought to be. Such seems now to be in the realm of possibility and should be completed in the immediate future.

In all there have been approximately fifty buildings constructed or replaced or undergoing major overhauling during these twenty-one years that I have served the Sunday School Board. Without exception, we have sought to build quality buildings. Too, we have paid for them as we have progressed.

Perhaps the building of all of these structures, although exceedingly expensive, was one of the easiest areas in which I have operated. Since I grew up in the building trade, I understand building processes. Too, I enjoyed watching structures taking shape. Other areas are harder because they are oftentimes invisible, and difficulties are much harder to handle then than those of visible forms such as brick and stone.

One of the most difficult areas in which I have functioned has been in the area of program correlation. For years the Convention had called for correlation of programs within the Sunday School Board. Also, I had asked that the Board correlate its programs with the missionary programs of the Woman's Missionary Union and Brotherhood. There have been sincere efforts to this end led by previous committees. It will never be achieved perfectly because of the complex organizational difficulties involved and the diversity of the people who demand different approaches.

Correlation—as we came to use the term—related to the process by which we purposely plan in such a way that various organizations such as Sunday School, Church Training, Woman's Missionary Union, the Brotherhood, and Church Music work together from earliest stages to provide balanced and harmonized programs for all.

This intercommunication of the agencies is made all the more difficult by virtue of the fact that the Brotherhood is located in Memphis and the Woman's Missionary Union in Birmingham. We have learned methods of overcoming the mileage distances and are carrying on communication not only within the framework of ongoing discussions, but much of the planning is done also in consultation with the mission boards and other agencies. In this way each can know exactly where the other is at all times in its programs and promotions.

The only real disappointment I've experienced in these years has been in our not being able to reach more people more rapidly. We have added hundreds of thousands, even millions, to the enrollment in these years, but I had hoped it would be twice that many.

While it has been tedious to do so, I have undertaken the writing of several books on request of certain departments. In these I have tried to meet specific needs in Southern Baptist life. Writing is never easy, for a person who does not have full time to give to it. It becomes virtually impossible when a person has to harmonize writing with administration. The very nature of administration is that it must stand ready to deal with problems when they arise. Without delay, the chief executive officer must make himself available any moment day or night so that the speediest possible solution can be found. This is

Trying to write a book or magazine article in this environment is awfully trying. At times it proves impossible. Writing needs to be done at a certain emotional level. That emotion increases as the manuscript progresses. The writing hopefully reaches its climax and then levels off toward a conclusion. If the writer is seeking to solve some aggravating problem while he is writing, his style will contain an up-and-down effect which does not reflect that smooth emotional flow. As a result the manuscript will tend to have a polka-dot nature in which expressed emotions are erratic. The manuscript will seem to ebb and flow or start and stop too often. Nevertheless, I have undertaken writing several books and have found joy in doing them.

One book was for a January Bible Study dealing with the Gospel of John under the title of *John's Witness to Jesus.* Another has been on polity dealing with how Baptists do things and why. One has dealt with the church, what it is trying to do and who the people are who constitute its membership. It was under the title *Your Life and Your Church.* Two were books that evolved from earlier writings I had done on a chapter-by-chapter basis for *Facts and Trends,* a publication designed to give early information and assistance to professional church workers. In that publication, I developed a column dealing with the philosophy and principles which seemed practical in the work. It was not an effort to be theological but philosophical in discussion. The first group of these writings were put together under the title *Memos on Christian Living.* Another came out later under the title *Reach Out.*

Because of the heavy work load I've had to carry, I've had to trust Miss Violet Medlin, my secretary, and Gomer Lesch in Public Relations to work with me, as well as some of the editors. In each case the content of these books was mine. I had dictated them in detail, but I would usually end up with twice or three times as much material as was needed for a book. I would reduce the content down to the appropriate length. At that point the ones named above would be invited to put the book into final shape for publication. This has been a rather routine process we have followed. In fact, only by this method have I been able to do the vast amount of writing I have undertaken over these two decades of hectic administrative pressures.

# 4
# Together We Have Labored

A study of historical incidents is interesting but people who brought those occurrences to pass are even more fascinating. Incidents do not simply happen. They are brought to pass. The record of the people who planned and produced the happenings with God's help make the most thrilling study of all. To deal with all of those who have influenced the life of the Board during my tenure would be impossible. Their number is legion, but I would like to include certain individuals who have made major contributions to the Board's growth in unique ways during my tenure.

No record of my years would be complete without words of praise for Dr. T. L. Holcomb, my predecessor, as chief executive officer of the institution. Southern Baptists will never know the depth of this man's ministry during the eighteen years he was here. Many feel, and I think justifiably, that the Convention would have split up and down the Mississippi River if Dr. Holcomb had not stepped into the breach just as and when he did to give the leadership needed. And he did it at great personal sacrifice.

Dr. Holcomb was pastor of the First Baptist Church of Oklahoma City. He was serving as a trustee of the Sunday School Board at the time of his election. He was not in the running for the office and did not wish to be the successor to Dr. I. J. Van Ness. It was conceded generally that Dr. J. O. Williams, business manager, was the one most apt to be the next executive secretary. As it turned out, a very ambitious and dynamic man from the eastern seaboard aspired to the job.

When it became obvious that Dr. J. O. could not counter the organized opposition of this aggressive man running for the office, Dr. Holcomb's name was introduced as a dark horse. He carried the day. Actually, Dr. Holcomb was not present at the time of his election. Mrs. Holcomb was bringing him to the Nashville meeting and they had a car wreck en route. He was with her in a distant hospital when he learned of his election. It took him considerable time and prayer to bring himself to the point of acceptance because he knew the weight of the responsibilities that would be thrust upon him immediately.

Fortunately, Dr. Holcomb was born east of the river in Mississippi but had served a number of years at Sherman, Texas, as pastor and also as executive secretary of the Baptist General Convention of Texas prior to going to Oklahoma. His leadership in the West had called attention to his abilities and promotional skills, his enthusiasm, and his power in speaking. And so he seemed to be the one person behind whom all Southern Baptists could unite. He stepped into the position to lead the denomination in an era of growth and expansion which was phenomenal in spite of wars, depressions, and hardships of every conceivable kind. It would be impossible to exaggerate the influence of his tenure and the impact of his ministry.

Dr. Holcomb did not consider himself an organizational man, yet he had the uncanny ability to inspire people to work together organizationally, uniting them behind definite goals and objectives which he clearly held before them. He found ways of working together in unity and harmony which helped consolidate the Convention.

The secretary in Dr. Holcomb's office served almost in an invisible way but she was a person who cannot be overlooked, either, if the record is to be complete. Miss Ethel Allen, who was my office secretary my first year in office, was in a position to know more of detail about the institution than any other living individual regardless of position held. Not only did Miss Allen serve my first year as my secretary but she had been the office secretary of Dr. T. L. Holcomb for the eighteen years of his tenure. She had served in the same capacity during the seventeen-year tenure of Dr. I. J. Van Ness. For eight years she was secretary to Dr. J. M. Frost, founder of the Sunday School Board. She was the one person whose life spanned most of the life of the institution. Her lovely manners and overflowing Christian spirit influenced many persons both inside and outside the Board during the course of her long tenure in the Executive Office where major actions were taken.

When Miss Allen approached retirement, we were faced with the tedious responsibility of discovering someone whose abilities, temperament, and age would qualify her as successor. Miss Violet Medlin, native of South Carolina, was discovered at a Sunday School enlargement campaign in Miami, Florida, and recommended to the post. These past twenty years have validated the wisdom of his choice. To serve as professional secretary in the office of a chief executive officer of an institution like the Sunday School Board is most demanding. Visitors from all over the world, learned as well as underprivileged, pass through the office. Each must be made to feel welcome with a sincerity that is genuine. Handling tedious correspondence on delicate issues, typing legal documents of utmost importance, working with Board committees in the early stages where discussions must be confidential, and being almost letter perfect in every field of endeavor is a requirement of the position. These qualifications have meshed in Miss Medlin's personality and services, and her contributions to the effectiveness of my tenure have been many.

Serving in a unique way so that his ministry to the Sunday School Board has overlapped mine almost in entirety has been J. M. Crowe. I brought him to the institution as administrative assistant. Later he was made associate executive secretary, then executive vice-president. While Dr. Crowe was born in Kentucky, he grew up in Southern Illinois—a strong Baptist area which has produced leadership for our Convention in amazing numbers. He had a background of serving both in Illinois and Missouri in the promotion of Sunday School and Training Union work prior to becoming educational director with C. C. Warren in the First Baptist Church of Charlotte, North Carolina. It was from that position that he came to be my associate in my last pastorate at the First Baptist Church of Abilene, Texas.

Our teaming up, however, was more than incidental. My bringing him to be my associate was actually a result of a resolution I had made when as a seminary student I watched him in action. I discovered that he was the one person whom I had met who supplemented me in every detail. Too, he was a man in whom I could have absolute confidence.

Dr. Crowe was not afraid to tackle any job anywhere at any time regardless of difficulty or complexity. Furthermore, he possesses a unique mind which operates as systematically as an electronic brain. He can file away details in organized fashion so that they are not only interrelated but can be called back with amazing speed and accuracy and without the bother of extended research. While he expects those working with and under him to do their best, he always respects their personalities and is totally fair in every relationship. I would not accept the request of the Board to be the new executive secretary in 1953 until members of the Board had expressed their willingness for me to bring J. M. Crowe as administrative assistant to handle the routines of daily operation in an institution already functioning on a nationwide basis.

Circumstances required that I be on the field a great deal of the time. While I was held responsible by Southern Baptists and the trustees for everything that went on in the institution, in no way could I personally supervise the multitudinous details of implementation in so many areas simultaneously and still travel the thousands of miles each month as the job required. Dr. Crowe's coming was a Godsend to me and the Board.

The coming of W. L. Howse as director of the Education Division bordered on miracle also. For twenty-one years he had taught in the field of religious education in our seminary in Fort Worth. Moreover, he had already been approached officially about succeeding J. M. Price who was approaching retirement. Because of a strange inner feeling he had, Dr. Howse had put off accepting the seminary's offer. At precisely this point we needed a person of his capabilities, background, and experience.

Dr. J. O. Williams, director of the Education and Promotion Division, had died and his post was vacant. Too, we wanted to lift Dr. Clifton J. Allen, head of the Editorial Division, to the post of editorial secretary so we could relate him officially to everything published by the Board. Dr. Allen's capabilities equipped him admirably for that responsibility. This left simultaneous vacancies in two of the divisions. By routine procedure, when vacancies occur on high level, we reexamine the organizational structure to see if it needs readjustment. Our study convinced us that these two divisions could be combined into an Education Division so we could better correlate the published materials with the planning and promotion of field programs.

Dr. Howse was the one man we found on the Baptist horizon who had exactly what Southern Baptists needed. Our committee of trustees agreed unanimously.

When we wired Dr. Howse, who was in St. Louis at the time on a field engagement, he agreed to see us. Never could he lay aside the conviction that the Lord wanted him at the Board for this one strategic responsibility, so he came. I doubt that any man ever did more precisely and flawlessly what he was employed to do as Dr. Howse did in this position, that of fusing two vast divisions into one unified operation moving toward a common objective. The fact is that if Dr. Howse had not accepted our offer, we likely would have been forced to go in another direction organizationally. He was the only man we knew who could do what he felt had to be done.

Dr. Allen Comish was brought into the Board life to succeed Dr. Howse upon retirement, with additional responsibilities in the publishing side of the institution's life. Not only did he come from the pastorate, but also with a doctorate in the field, several years of experience in the Sunday School Department with Dr. Barnette, and a tenure as chairman of the Church Services and Materials Committee of the Board as a trustee. His task was to move the earlier developments in education, which were valid theologically and educationally, more toward simplicity in expression and promotion so the people at the grass roots could better understand and support what we were trying to accomplish. This was to be done without any compromises educationally and philosophically. The response given Dr. Comish's leadership in this direction has been encouraging, even thrilling.

The role which capable and dedicated women have played in the Sunday School Board's life is greater than the average Baptist can comprehend. In fact, the institution could not operate without the women who work here. They are as capable and committed as any of the male employees. They give of their time just as sacrificially, spending endless hours and days on the road traveling the nation

50

GOD IS MY RECORD

over trying to help churches in struggling situations do a better job in Bible teaching and membership training.

Although the men usually are the ones who emerge in the limelight, receiving the headlines through the public media and maybe in recorded history, it cannot be forgotten that at least two-thirds of the employees of the Sunday School Board are women. Many of them hold high professional positions with some in management roles. To illustrate, the place Miss Annie Ward Byrd has played in curriculum development and manuscript analysis is historic. I think of the influence of Mrs. Edith Walker in Church Architecture and in the design of church buildings, and the impact of the women managers of Baptist Book Stores.

Women have climbed high in the life of the institution. Still they have not moved up in the organizational line as much as I have personally desired. Certainly it is not because they lack ability or commitment. As the psychology of Southern Baptists changes so as to allow larger roles of leadership for women in local church life—which is the present trend—women will find their highest potential at the Board. Because churches themselves require men in certain roles of church leadership and responsibility and are sometimes reluctant for such positions to be given to women employees, the denomination's institutions are held back. But this is changing and should.

An illustration of what women can do was shown by Mrs. Agnes Durant Pylant. She was deliberately chosen as a department head because we felt a woman could do a better job there at the time than a man could do. History has proved we were right. In the light of existing circumstances and vocal opposition at the time, we wondered for a time if anyone could do that job acceptably. We brought her to establish the Church Recreation Department. Many were opposed to recreation as such and loudly said so. Too, the standards of church recreation were very diverse in different parts of the country, so national standards were not easy to determine and establish.

Perhaps no two persons ever have been more different than J. N. Barnette and J. E. Lambdin, and yet these two men have had as much influence on the life and growth of Southern Baptists as any other men in the past generation. J. N. Barnette was truly a charismatic leader, in the true meaning of the Greek *charisma*. He possessed the warm personality and leadership skills that called him to the attention of any group the moment he walked into a room. While he did not possess the physical attractiveness of John L. Hill, Broadman book editor, who was as handsome as a Greek god, and therefore was virtually idolized by men and women, J. N. Barnette was still a natural leader who dedicated his abilities totally to the Lord's work.

Barnette proved his abilities while he was still a farmer in North Carolina serving as superintendent of a little Sunday School in a rural church. His accomplishments there were so many and so consistent that the attention of the entire state was called to his achievements. As a result he came to work for a while with the state forces in Sunday School promotion. Then he was brought to the Sunday School Board in Nashville in the area of associational work. He went from that post to head the Sunday School Department and be responsible for the promotion of Bible teaching through Sunday Schools the nation over. Barnette was the sort of person who could work all day and be just as effervescent and enthusiastic at the end of the day as he was at the beginning. He could take a successful Bible teaching program being carried out in some remote church and make every person in the Convention feel that he, too, could achieve the same type of bold accomplishments. He had only to apply himself and lead his people and to do so upon returning home. Especially was this true at Ridgecrest and Glorieta, where the inspiration which Dr. Barnette generated reached back into the remotest areas of the land in promotion of Sunday School work. Glorious history was written thereby for Southern Baptists.

The crowning achievement under Dr. Barnette's leadership was the "Million More in '54" campaign which was in full swing shortly after my arrival at the Sunday School Board. While the movement did not reach a total of a million additional people, it did produce the most rapid growth known to Southern Baptist Sunday Schools. It surged us upward to become the largest Sunday School movement of recorded religious history. The advance of the Bible teaching program helped move forward every other area of the denomination's work, including training and evangelism, church music and study courses. Thus, the denomination received a thrust as a result of the spirited leadership of J. N. Barnette who believed ardently in the educational and organizational principles laid down by Arthur Flake. In fact he built his ministry upon Flake's concept of building churches, and led his successor A. V. Washburn to do the same.

J. E. Lambdin had qualities in other areas. While he did not have the platform skills of J. N. Barnette he was a persistent plodder who planned details with thoroughness. His real genius, however, was in the selection of personnel. He was a wizard in evaluating persons. In fact he surrounded himself with some of the most capable workers in denominational life today. He trained them with such thoroughness as they worked with him that they're now holding top-level positions in every seminary, board agency, and area of denominational life. Some of the best Southern Baptist leaders were first discovered in odd places by J. E. Lambdin. He saw them as diamonds in the rough, discovering abilities in them which they had never discovered in themselves. He was able to nurture those latent abilities into fullest expression. He not only had the ability to pick people with potential skills, but he had also possessed the wisdom of having them in the right places doing the right job at the right time. It is uncanny how efficient he was in this area of personnel selection and placement which had to be largely judgmental in nature. Steps in this area had to be taken in faith because many times the people had not been tested in areas of heavy responsibility which he placed on them. It is miraculous how often he won out. By these processes he built a training program second to none with God's help and laid the ground-work for Philip B. Harris and his associates to expand and deepen training programs.

In discussing how we have labored together, I would be untrue to truth and to myself if I did not magnify the contribution of the Negro employees to the Sunday School Board. Some of the best loved and most respected employees of the institution have been black people. They have served with sacrificial devotion and commitment, sensing the call of the Lord to areas of assignment given them.

Henry Lee Kage worked for the Board for forty-seven years. Having come in his teens, he worked until retirement. He had an unusual type mind that could remember every plane schedule and train schedule in and out of Nashville. For years he was in essence the transportation clerk, handling the securing of tickets to every nook and cranny of this nation for field workers trying to get to "that last church" to help them do a better job. He knew every person at the Board by name. He was absolutely honest and almost flawless in his remembrance of even the minutest details. He purchased automobile tags annually to keep our people from having to stand in line by the hour at the courthouse to do so. He handled the delivery of telegrams and important matters. Most of all he handled huge sums of money for daily deposit. No bank president has ever had a higher record of honesty and efficiency. Henry Lee is the type of person who has helped exalt the work of the Sunday School Board even though he himself was never a member of a Southern Baptist church. Still, his commitment to Southern Baptists was beyond question and was outstanding.

The Sunday School Board has tried to be fair to the blacks during their employment. In fact the institution pioneered in several areas— charting courses for other institutions to follow in their employment practices and treatment of persons of minority races.

One of the first things done after we came to the Board in 1953 was to issue the direction that we were going to pay by job description. People doing comparable work would receive the same amount of pay regardless of who they were or where they came from.

We never received any complaints when the blacks began receiving the same pay as the whites when they did the same work. Oddly enough, we almost had a revolution when we started paying the women as much as the men under the same circumstances. Nevertheless, we stayed by our decision, and rode through the vocal obstacles confronting us. This we have never retracted or regretted. Our actions were ahead of all federal laws in this regard. We feel this is the way it should be. Christianity should lead the way.

We put in one of the first integrated industrial cafeterias in the state of Tennessee. Only two complaints were received and they were from retired preachers who were working temporarily at the Board in order to become eligible for Social Security. Each of them said,

"We know you're doing the right thing, but we're just not used to its being done this way." Everyone else has supported the idea from the first.

These efforts of fairness toward all persons paid off, although this was not even remotely in our minds at the time. When the Sunday School Board was under attack from extreme racial activists who were trying to pressure the Board to coerce the churches of the Southern Baptist Convention into an all-out program of integration in one fell swoop, the blacks stepped in to defend our position, spirit, and approach. Knowing that under Baptist polity individual churches had to make up their own minds on this matter, we had rejected the idea of extreme radical activism. Therefore we were under severe attack from activists. It was then that the blacks working at the Sunday School Board stepped in, silenced the criticism by denying that there was any justification for such aggressive attacks. They contended with their own people that the criticisms were wholly unjustified. They pointed out that the Sunday School Board was doing vastly more than most institutions of the nation and was doing so without creating issues or ill feelings on the part of anyone.

When the time came to select someone for a managerial position in the shipping area of the Operations Building, we tested a number of employees. Discovering that one of our black workers had the highest qualifications, we employed him for the job. Even though we wondered at the time if some of the white persons working in that area might be reluctant to accept it and work under a black supervisor, we nevertheless proceeded to put him in that high position of responsibility. It is complimentary to the workers of the Sunday School Board that not one person left his job because there was a black supervisor. Nor have we heard one voice of criticism inside or out because we took such a step. It was the right thing to do. We were willing to live with any criticisms that might come. Fortunately they did not.

One of the men who has helped me tremendously to be ready for my job at the Sunday School Board was my former teacher, Dr. Gaines S. Dobbins. I perhaps quote him more often than any teacher under whom I ever studied. We have had a close relationship with his family because Mrs. Dobbins and my mother were desk mates in the same little country school in south Mississippi as small girls. They grew up together and graduated together. Therefore we have had very deep appreciation for each other although we as families have not had too many direct contacts because many miles have separated us. I admired Dr. Dobbins in his teaching years. He was so thorough both as a scholar and as a teacher. I came to appreciate him all the more after I came to the Sunday School Board and found how willing he was to fit into any assignment we wanted him to take. His analyses, judgments, and recommendations have been virtually without flaw.

Even though Dr. Dobbins is known as a teacher and has spent most of his life in that field—at Louisville and then for a decade at Golden Gate Seminary—he served remarkably in other fields as well. He was a skilled pastor in his young years and then came to the Sunday School Board in an editorial role prior to his seminary responsibilities of instruction. This prepared him in a peculiar way for a role of leadership in the Baptist World Alliance. He was the man of the hour at the very hour he was needed to stress Bible teaching and membership training on a worldwide basis. Because of his age and record of performance he was heard with respect and appreciation. Because of his sheer mastery of the field of education he was followed with gladness. I can think of no other man who could have done what Dr. Dobbins did in world Baptist circles like and when he did it. It could well be that this worldwide impact on Baptist life in helping set up the Commission on Teaching and Training and getting its work going in the Baptist World Alliance will be recorded in history as his greatest Christian contribution.

Although I never studied under W. W. Barnes, the historian, his evaluations and judgments have meant much to me also. My first discussions with him grew out of my compliment of his book recording the history of the first hundred years of Southern Baptists. When I told him that he had not only written with accuracy but with clarity while making his history sound like a romance, his reply was, "I hope it is accurate but you are aware that historians are never sure, aren't you?" When I appeared startled at his statement, he gave an interesting explanation.

He asked me if I had ever been secretary of an organization. I told him I had been. He asked me then if I put into the minutes a record of any personal arguments growing out of individual differences which showed up in business meetings when they had no relationship whatsoever to the subject under discussion. I told him that I never inserted such things in the minutes. He replied that historians, therefore, are writing from an inadequate record, even though what they write is validated by minutes and records. He stressed that minutes do not tell the whole story of any happenings. Dr. Barnes went on to explain that there is a tremendous difference between actuality and appearance. Every historian is faced with an aggravating dilemma as he tries to make a distinction between the two.

He related an incident to illustrate what he was talking about. Dr. Barnes and his son had gone to Ridgecrest. Immediately his son was fascinated by trees and mountains and was roaming the hills. Shortly he rushed back to say to his father: "There's the funniest snake up there I ever saw. He has two mouths, four eyes, and legs on the side of his head." His father, thinking that the son's imagination had run wild, chided him for describing a nonexistent type snake. The boy was not threatened by his dad's rebuttals, but said, "Come on and I will show him to you." Dr. Barnes, thinking that he would back the boy down, went with him to the foot of a tree up the mountainside. Said Dr. Barnes: "There was the snake exactly as the boy had described him. He had two mouths, four eyes, legs on the side of his head—but it was a snake—swallowing a frog." The snake had left just enough of the frog visible that he had two mouths, four eyes, and legs on the side of his head.

Dr. Barnes explained that often there will be a million miles of difference between appearance and reality. This is the bane of existence of a historian. Barnes went on to explain that during my tenure as executive secretary of the Sunday School Board I might feel at times that Baptist state paper editors, for instance, were the most inaccurate of writers. "They will attack you frequently and fiercely," he said, "when you know that the attacks are unjustified. It will help you keep calm under such attacks if you will only remember that there is a lot of difference between appearance and reality. Baptist editors do not have the facts. They are too far away. Therefore, they have to write on the basis of appearance. Many of their writings will be woefully inaccurate. Don't feel that they are falsifying when this occurs. It will help you to remember that they are writing without having true facts before them. They are writing about things as they see them from afar. This you must remember." How many times it has been so.

Dr. Barnes went on to elaborate further by saying that perhaps the most difficult problems I would face would be when Southern Baptist Convention messengers confused appearances with reality. "When they do," he said, "they are apt to take matters in their own hands from the trustees and make trustee decisions on the floor of the Convention. As they do, they are apt to act on appearance and not on fact. If done," he explained, "it may take the Convention a quarter of a century to correct its error. But they will in time," he added. "We must be willing to accept this as one of the prices we pay for maintaining our democratic processes." There have been a few times I have seen this happen. Actions were taken on what appeared to be facts but those appearances were far removed from the actual situation. Sincerity does not help when this does occur.

Likewise there are times when a messenger speaks on the Convention floor, giving the appearance of unselfish motivation, when all the time his discussion is motivated by a bit of hidden agenda. Some individuals have ego needs which seem to be met only by addressing a Convention in debate or by presenting a resolution. One debater I recall owed a long-standing debt to the Baptist Book Store, and spoke vociferously against the Sunday School Board on an unrelated issue. Decisions based on Convention actions need to take all these facets into consideration.

What makes it even more difficult for the Convention to work out details of institutional administration on the floor of the Convention is that institutions are assigned specific and oftentimes technical areas in which the average person is untrained to even identify the real problem as it exists. It needs also to be remembered that 85 percent

James L. Sullivan—six months old

The birthplace of James Sullivan—Silver Creek, Lawrence County, Mississippi, March 12, 1910

(Top) James Washington Sullivan, Brother Arthur, James, and Mary Ellen Dampeer Sullivan (1913)

(Below—left to right) James (8), Edith (less than 1), and Arthur (9)—posed in 1918

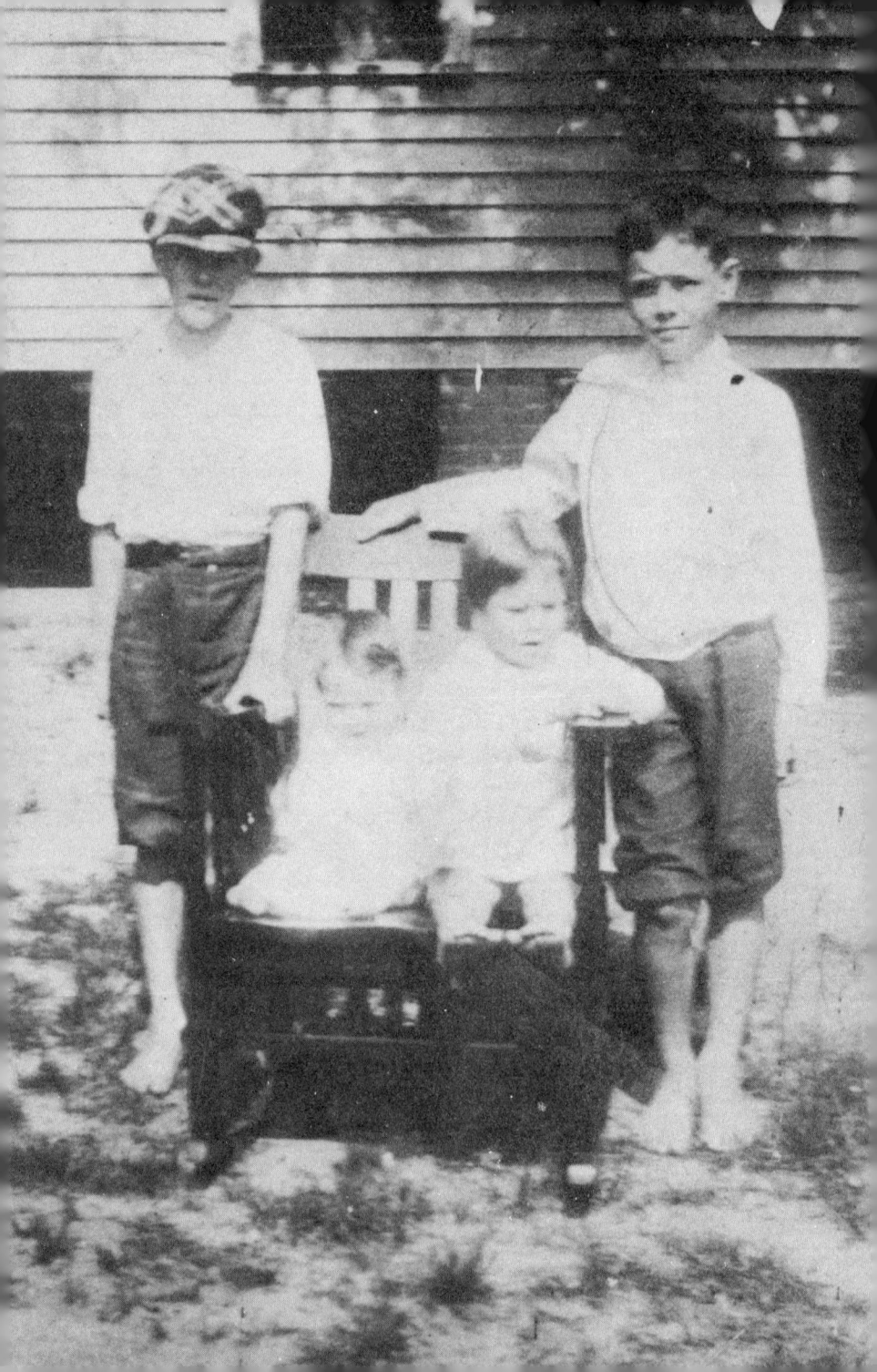

(Opposite page) As the Sullivan "tribe" increased, Hilan (second from left) was added to (left to right) Arthur, Edith, and James (ca. 1920 or 1921).

(Above) Arthur and James in 1925 or 1926

(Above) James L. Sullivan, football star at Mississippi College

(Opposite page) The Mississippi College Choctaws (Coach Stanley Robinson—fifth from left), James L. Sullivan (second from right)

**Mississippi College and the University of Mexico football teams in front of the U.S. Embassy, Mexico City (1929)**

**Seminarian Sullivan at Southern Seminary (1932-1935)**

**Sullivan at Beaver Dam, Kentucky, where he pastored from 1933-1939**

(Above) At Brookhaven, Mississippi (1946) are (left to right) Lynn, Velma, David, James, and Beth.

Dr. Sullivan about the time of his move from Belmont Heights Church, Nash.

Dr. Sullivan with Dr. J. Marvin Crowe and Miss Violet Medlin

James and Velma Sullivan,
partners for forty years

Dr. Sullivan and one of his "confidants"

**Passing on "Sullivan's Hollow" lore to two of his grandsons**

**Granddad with his fellow-mariners**

Portrait of Dr. Sullivan which hangs outside of the Van Ness Auditorium at
the Board

of the persons who register at the Southern Baptist Convention are preachers, yet the Sunday School Board is expected to minister to "the average church." There is no church in the Southern Baptist Convention made up of 85 percent preachers. Therefore the Board can be doing exactly what the churches have asked and yet find itself in difficulty with the Convention because the Convention itself is not typical of the churches the Board is set up to serve. This is why the trustee system must be trusted. This is why administration of boards, agencies, and institutions simply must be carried on by the trustees who are expected to operate under it in carrying out the guidelines of the Convention. Whenever the Convention assumes the role of trusteeship directly, it is apt to make blunders that may take decades to correct. Dr. Barnes' comments helped me to understand this fact and be more patient when they did occur. And they have.

In my early days at the Sunday School Board I had thought and hoped that we could set up an organizational structure that would endure throughout my entire tenure in office so I would not have to go through headaches of constant reorganization. Such was not to be.

I discovered to my surprise that organization is not and can never be static. It has to be constantly changing. It is better to adjust parts of it with frequency than it is to go a long number of years and have to make a massive change of everything simultaneously, making upheavals unavoidable internally and externally.

The Board's employees have worked as a team, but the team has demanded constant updating and restructuring to carry a rapidly increasing volume and load.

# 5
# Upsurge in a Youthful Convention

There is a close parallel between the physical growth of a person and the unfolding development of a convention. This principle not only holds true of state conventions but applies to the Southern Baptist Convention as well.

As conventions have begun, they have started usually on such a low level of weakness that there was the question even of survival. State conventions were begun generally by Southern Baptist people who had moved into another geographical area. They wanted the same type of worship service, educational program, and mission promotion that they had known back home where Southern Baptists have predominated. So a group of them would cluster together, start as a Sunday School or prayer meeting, and a church would soon be underway. In turn they would begin talking immediately about starting mission points elsewhere. In ways that seem impossible, new missions would be begun and supported through the sacrifice and dedication of loyal workers of some nearby mission congregation. Soon a cluster of churches was underway. When this cluster would become large enough to function together, the churches would organize a fellowship. Eventually out of that fellowship would evolve a state convention.

The Southern Baptist Convention does not select representatives from a state convention to serve on its boards unless twenty-five thousand church members exist within that state. Still everyone has worked toward helping that small group attain a position of maturity which would make representation possible on boards and agencies of the Convention. Through this process of growth and development, our Convention has covered the entire geographical area of our nation. Although in some sections of the country the Baptists of several states cooperate in what we call a state convention organization, still the purposes of conventions are carried out.

The Southern Baptist Convention agencies function "in the territory of the United States and its possessions." This is significant. These small Baptist organizations in the beginning seemed helpless. Others would join in to assist them in discovering personnel, training their people, building their buildings, carrying on their work, and doing all the things necessary to build a Baptist constituency. But this has been done in such a way and with the speed that has amazed other religious bodies. Units of organization thus built have become vigorous with abundant energy standing ready to undertake tasks of any size. Such a spirit has helped build a vigorous convention, bustling and growing. By this process the Southern Baptist Convention has become the largest evangelical denomination of a nation. Really its potential is just now beginning to be realized throughout the nation.

Baptist bodies at the beginning often must be dealt with as though they were infants, helpless, and crying for assistance. As they have grown, they have taken on the temperament of a larger child and then a youth. It is significant how they have had to learn how to get along with each other and with others. They have had to learn how to be sympathetic and cooperative and develop the art of giving and taking in democratic processes.

With the passing of years, a state convention in a new geographical area begins to take on the attitude of a more mature youth. It has more energy than it knows how to handle. It will often undertake projects beyond its ability. It is optimistic, dynamic, daring, and at times even brash.

The next developing stage is that of a young adult. It becomes more mature in thinking, balanced in judgment, vigorous in action, and ready to take any type of worthwhile dare for the sake of God. Its future is still ahead of it. It is at this stage that a state convention comes into its own as its work becomes stabilized.

Alas, some state conventions occasionally develop old age symptoms. They become sluggish in actions, slow in movements, lose ambition, and see a diminishing growth pattern which causes concern of everyone. Responses are very much like a person of age with sluggish muscles and arthritic joints.

My own classification would be that the Southern Baptist Convention is just now hitting its older youth period. As religious bodies are measured, the Southern Baptist Convention is still young. This explains some of the actions which are expressions of immaturity that are often difficult for newspaper men or commentators of religious affairs to understand adequately. Because they do not understand the Southern Baptist Convention nature and terminology, often they mislead their readers in their interpretations and news reports.

I was impressed with the youthfulness of the Southern Baptist Convention when I went to speak at a meeting of the Historical Society in South Carolina. A plaque was being unveiled identifying the location of Elford Print Shop which produced the first printed materials under Southern Baptist Convention authorization in 1863 with Dr. Basil Manly, Jr., as editor.

Dr. Manly had participated in the founding of our first theological seminary, which was begun in Greenville and was later moved to Louisville, Kentucky. He was in his forties during the Civil War. Being a man of vision and dedication, he joined other capable Baptist leaders. Together they produced printed materials far ahead of their day. The finances of the Civil War, however, caused bankruptcy of this effort but such does not take away from the glory of what these men did for Southern Baptists on a massive scale.

At this historical meeting in Greenville, South Carolina, a few years ago, two of the children of Dr. Basil Manly, Jr., appeared as honor guests. Children of this founder of our oldest seminary and editor of our Convention's first printed materials attended the meeting honoring their father. Such points up the youthfulness of our Convention, its desire to see progress, its look to the future, its willingness to undertake challenging endeavors, and at times the experiencing of actions which imply that more maturity is needed at certain points.

It is hoped that this youthful psychology will not diminish or disappear. It is this resilience and spirit which has been one of the greatest attributes of the Convention. This has helped it attain a position of leadership in the religious life of the world with some of the largest theological schools, education and publishing developments, largest mission efforts, and greatest numerical growth known to religious history.

This spirit of youth has shown itself in many ways. One is in the willingness to undertake vast movements which bring concerted efforts on the part of the people toward common goals. This was true of the "Million More in '54" movement which was an effort to reach the largest number of people for Bible study we have ever reached in our history. Such was accomplished even though we did not reach the ultimate numerical goal set. The 30,000 Movement under the leadership of C. C. Warren, a former president of the Convention, was an effort to establish new churches in every area of the Convention where churches were needed and people could be located. This movement was spearheaded by the Home Mission Board and the Sunday School Board working in joint endeavor. And while thirty thousand new places of worship were not developed, a host of new churches and missions were established. Many of the people being reached and taught today were enlisted through those new units begun in Southern Baptist life through movements such as this.

The Convention has always tried to stay alert to the needs of the people. It has been willing to move into new geographical areas speedily to try to help accomplish things considered pressing needs. As we have reached large numbers of people, there were those among them who were unusual people either with remarkable advantages or disadvantages, talent or limitations. The Convention began to assume responsibility for educating disadvantaged and unusual people as well as the brilliant and talented.

The first effort was toward those without hearing. We discovered that the vocabulary of a deaf person was quite different from that of a hearing person. Abstract terms were to be avoided. Deaf individuals can understand words that are concrete in nature, so we developed a quarterly of such words for their benefit. It was discovered by specialists as they analyzed this quarterly that we could alter it some and use it also for the newly literate. We secured the assistance of Dr. Laubach in the development and expansion of our publication. We changed the title from *Sunday School Lessons for the Deaf* to *Sunday School Lessons Simplified*. We enlarged the usefulness of the publication because there were many people being reached who could not even sign their names. Churches were even trying to teach persons to read and write in underprivileged areas. Our materials proved most helpful in such situations.

As churches developed, the leadership needed assistance. They needed to know how to develop church programs and administer them from a leadership position. *Church Administration* was thus made available as a magazine of special assistance to those in general church leadership. An effort was made to enlist the masses of a church congregation in a constant reading program. Church libraries were established by the thousands over the Convention, and a new magazine *The Church Library* was begun to guide in this effort and become a focal point of attention and instruction. Church libraries now cover audiovisual and other assignments and the publication is known as *Media: Library Services Journal.*

With the increase of free time as limited working hours in America became prevalent, *Church Recreation,* begun as a new magazine to help meet this need, was a unique approach and service.

Book store expansion was undertaken. Studies were made to make sure that materials and supplies could be put in the hands of church leaders as needed without undue delay. Efforts were put forth to place Baptist Book Stores at strategic distribution sites where materials could be gotten quickly to the churches, for educational materials to them are as necessary as brick and stone to the contractor. Without proper equipment any worker is handicapped in doing his job. Therefore, the denomination sought to meet this need in a practical way by making a nationwide study and operating the maximum number of stores that could carry their own financial weight while fulfilling this denominational responsibility. Some of the stores were unable to carry themselves financially and had to be subsidized, some quite heavily, but it was done gladly by the denomination for the sake of the churches where needs were most acutely felt.

In some of the newer states where Baptist strength had not reached a sufficient level for them to own and operate Baptist buildings in which they could house their state Baptist offices, the Sunday School Board stepped in to provide buildings for them in a unique business arrangement. The state convention would buy the land. We would build a building. Then we would locate the Baptist Book Store in their building. With rent the book store paid, the indebtedness against the building was financed over an agreed number of years. The building then, as well as the land, would belong to that state convention. By that time, it was hoped, the convention had reached a position of strength where it could improve the building, enlarge it, or relocate it.

For a long time most of our Baptist Book Stores were in or adjacent to the state Baptist buildings. Recently the trends have been in the opposite direction, because so many Baptist buildings have moved into the suburbs or rural sections. Of course retail operations by Baptist Book Stores have not been able to move. Buyers prefer that we locate in a retail section of the city so they can buy from the Baptist Book Stores when they are making purchases from other sales outlets. This trend is moving us toward major shopping centers.

We may be facing another rather drastic change in book stores. It deals with the new United States government postal areas and system of mail distribution. It may mean that in the future we will have to give more special attention to the Baptist Book Store location to speed up distribution of church supplies by mail order. Otherwise, packages may go two hundred miles only to be resorted and sent back over the same road to get to the customer who may live on the other side of a Baptist Book Store from which mailing was done in the first place. We have yet to learn what this will do to our book store operations, but the Convention can be assured that the stores' leadership will do that which seems best in the light of all involvements.

With constant and rapid growth the Sunday School Board had to adequately equip itself for the handling of many materials simultaneously in one place. We preferred a widespread place where we could operate with conveyor chains or electric carts and hoists where most everything could be handled in bulk without having to be lifted or shifted by human hands.

The answer seemed to be the erection of a massive Operations Building. We were finally able to undertake this when we secured property from the local railroad where a railroad freight house had long been located. This has enabled us to operate far more economically and have more stock on hand in such a way that it could be handled with speed and efficiency as well as economy. This has been a lifesaving development although it was very expensive with the construction of a building of such size that the roof could be used as a parking building and with two floors underneath for the handling of merchandise. The second floor is for the handling of materials for book stores and trade outlets. The ground floor for church literature and curriculum materials that were shipped on systematic schedules.

Southern Baptist growth forced additional seminaries. In each instance, the Convention has asked agencies to sacrifice a part of their earnings to help get the new institution started and underway. Because of the apparent needs and the Convention actions, this has been done.

With the beginning of each new seminary, the Sunday School Board was asked to make a contribution, usually of some $50,000. In addition, we usually provided a children's building or some other building. Under the same system by which we would finance Baptist Book Stores, we would pay off the building debt by book store rental of the campus stores. This enabled us to have a store at a proper location. It also enabled the seminary to have an additional building which usually became a children's building or one for general religious education purposes.

The Department of Church Architecture had to undergo tremendous changes and enlargement because of the number of buildings that were being erected by churches the nation over. This department covers the major part of two floors in the Tower Building. Its men are specialists in the field and deal with unique problems churches face in their building programs. This department designs free of charge for the churches the best possible layout according to the educational and worship needs. One of the services is to send consultants from Nashville to help churches at strategic times, suggesting ways in which they may get the maximum building for the smallest amount of money.

The sacrificial service of W. A. Harrell got this department operating full scale. In the early days, the Department of Church Architecture helped churches with plans and programs for the financing of their building operations and for the assistance in denominational mission projects. The department would help the churches with their building fund plans whereby they would suggest the type of building a congregation of that size and location ought to erect and ways in which they might finance it in the light of all circumstances involved. Of course, each situation was different. Some of the churches would undertake projects far too big in which it was apparent that they were undertaking the impossible. One of the functions of the Church Architecture Department has been to show churches what they can and cannot afford and how to finance the building without jeopardizing their future seriously.

It was during this period of expansion and rapid growth that we separated Convention Press from Broadman Press. Their modes of operation would be different. Both of them would still be ours, and production processes would remain somewhat the same but the method of payment to the author and the distribution of the product would be quite different.

We noticed that books which were developed to meet the educational needs of churches distributed the greatest number of copies. Titles and content would be predetermined by curriculum specialists at the Board who would want to fulfill certain needs with certain books. This was true especially of study course books which dealt with methodology, doctrine, or some specialized area where churches wished their members to give concentrated attention to a particular need in the church situation or calendar. Circulation did not depend necessarily on who the author was, how creative he was, or how much work he had done on the development of the manuscript. Circulation was tied more closely to the subject matter and how it related to the overall educational program of the denomination. It was felt, therefore, that a flat fee rather than royalty should be paid for such a book.

Everything was quite different from a Broadman book in which an author would by his own imagination and creativity develop the content of a book. Then he would write it in detail. We decided that the latter type production was one for which royalty should be paid on the basis of circulation. These would be books of general nature and would be distributed through many outlets.

As an illustration, *Building a Standard Sunday School* would be developed and distributed through Baptist Book Stores only. It would be addressed specifically to Baptist people and would deal with methods that would meet the needs of churches. That would be a Convention Press book. By contrast, a book on prayer would be of interest to people of other denominations or of no denomination. It would be produced under Broadman Press imprint and would be distributed not only through our Baptist Book Stores but through thousands of other distribution centers so as to give the book the widest possible geographical circulation. It would have a different type of advertisement as well as a different type of distribution method.

The growth of the Southern Baptist Convention has inspired growth in other Baptist groups. It was during this period of vast expansion that an invitation came asking me to go to Japan to assist the Foreign Mission Board in some of their mission educational projects. I could not go myself and sent Dr. W. L. Howse, director of the Education Division, in my place. It was providential. He not only did work in Japan which was historic, but was able to expand his journey to Australia and New Zealand. We were able to help the Baptist brethren there through a transition period and help them start all-age Sunday Schools.

At the same time, we were able through the Baptist World Alliance to be instrumental in the setting up of a Commission on Bible Teaching and Membership Training which would accelerate Bible teaching the world over where it has not been developed up until that time.

The growth pattern of Southern Baptists brought some unexpected things we had not anticipated. Opposition from anti-religious people began to be heard because they could not tolerate the growth of religious bodies. This means we were under attack. Independent churches also made every sort of attack against the Sunday School Board to try to forestall its growth, but without success. One point of attack was the Uniform Lesson Series in which Southern Baptists developed their sequence of Sunday School lessons in cooperation with other evangelical denominations, a process which has continued for a century. After sequences of Scripture study had been agreed upon, the participating denominations would then write their own lessons in detail for their own people. In this manner they would be most effective.

In the beginning the Uniform Lesson Series was not copyrighted. As time passed, however, some denominationalists and some non-denominationalists wanted to take the lesson courses and use them against the denominations which had developed them. It was necessary to copyright them. Opponents attacked the system, feeling that it was a compromise somehow on the part of Southern Baptists to work with other denominations, even though the opponents did not know any details. Therefore they kept some denominations under ruthless attack. Several times the Sunday School Board made depth studies. Each time the trustees were unanimous in their feeling that this was the best way of developing Sunday School lesson courses. They stated with clarity and conviction that there is no compromise of any kind because we still controlled every word of every lesson and came to the work with nothing but the Bible in hand. The materials were ours, although the Scriptures were the same as those on which other denominations were making studies at the same time.

With the growth of the denomination, we had to develop a new series of lesson courses to allow for coordinated program planning. The Life and Work Series thus came into existence. It is planned jointly with all existing organizations in a Baptist church in order that more systematic efforts might be made toward coordination. History proves that churches are divided about evenly in their selection of materials, with half choosing the Uniform and half the Life and Work lessons. Larger churches seem to prefer Life and Work because of correlation. Both are ours and we work diligently preparing each.

Growth in Southern Baptist life brought additional problems for us to deal with. As we began to expand in size and territorial services, we had to have more facilities, equipment, properties, and inventories. This immediately raised the question of taxation with the local governments where we have operated. The Nashville properties, which is the major center of our operation, have had two experiences with city assessments, both of which have gone to the state Supreme Court before settlement. Some citizens feel we ought to pay taxes on all of our properties because we are not strictly a church. Therefore they feel we should not be exempt from property taxes in the city of Nashville. Others take the opposite view.

We have been sympathetic with the city's financial problem because approximately 40 percent of its total assessed evaluation is on the tax exempt roll. Nashville is a city of colleges, government buildings, institutions of learning, churches, welfare organizations, and such like. This, however, did and does not change the law and does not change the principle which we felt gave exemption to the Sunday School Board in the first place. We do not object to paying taxes on parking lots, cafeteria, rental properties, and any other type of operation which is not clearly related to the charter purpose of the institution. It is different on space used for Bible teaching and church membership training programs and activities that exist for the purpose of expanding the kingdom of God.

We once debated moving to a suburban location. We went so far at one time as to buy an option on 120 acres where the 100 Oaks Shopping Center is now located. Had we relocated then we might not have had quite the problem with taxation, but we chose to stay in the downtown area. Our choice was deliberate and we think intelligent. The nature of our operation and the peculiar needs of the personnel who work for us seem to make this mandatory.

The laws of Tennessee have been based not on use or nonuse of church property, but on "purpose of use." This makes the approach different fundamentally. Many state Supreme Court decisions clearly set forth this philosophy. This is why a restaurant on a college campus selling to students does not pay taxes but a restaurant on the main street up town selling for profit does.

One of our difficulties in finding a legal base that would apply to all religious groups is that certain denominations like the Church of Christ, lacking a central nationwide organization, must look to independent publishers for educational materials. They do pay taxes and express intense feeling that Baptists and Methodists do not. Actually, their publishing operations are privately owned. They are stock companies and earnings from their operations are distributed to stockholders, making them clearly taxable. At the same time,

Baptists and Methodists own their operation. There are no stockholders. There are no divisions of earnings. Their work is religious in nature and deals with the propagation of the gospel. Historically, therefore, they have been declared tax exempt on properties related to their charter purposes.

The Supreme Court of Tennessee seems now to be trying to broaden the Board's tax base. Their most recent decision calls on us to pay on properties not used for our charter purposes plus those used for production and distribution of *general* religious materials. Space used to produce and distribute *institutional* materials is exempt. If the latter materials are interpreted as Baptist-related, we are still left with a serious legal problem concerning outreach materials designed to propagate the gospel among non-Christians.

The question of taxation was raised at the state level at Ridgecrest and Glorieta. In each case, decisions were favorable to the Sunday School Board on somewhat the same basis on which Nashville properties have until now been declared taxable or exempt. That is, taxes are paid on barber shops, beauty parlors, gift shops, washateria, and the like, but not on the areas where the Word of God is taught and religious principles are expounded.

Perhaps the most complex tax problem was in the state of Oregon, where they placed what they called an income tax on our nationwide operation because we had a small store in Portland. We were subsidizing it heavily. Under Oregon law they did not merely tax the business operation within the state. They taxed the nationwide operation because we had an outlet in Oregon. Feeling the injustice of such an approach, we moved the store into the state of Washington rather than submit to what we considered a totally unfair tax system.

In addition to tax problems, the growth of the Sunday School Board also raised the question of labor unions. Labor organizers have sought on several occasions to organize certain groups of workers within the institution, especially workers doing manual labor in the Operations Building. Only once did these labor agitators succeed in bringing the matter to an election. Even then the employees voted it down. The last time they tried to organize was when Jimmy Hoffa was desperately seeking to organize all religious publishing houses in Nashville simultaneously, both blacks and whites.

While we have never taken a position for or against labor unions, we do feel they do have a definite place when properly operated and administered. We have not felt that they were necessary at the Sunday School Board where we have sought to be Christian in every relationship. We have studiously worked against any type of sweat-shop conditions. We have tried to keep salaries abreast of institutions from which our employees are secured. We have sought to increase wages according to the cost of living index, making periodic studies of what is happening to the American dollar and adjusting salaries accordingly. We have also tried to stay ahead of the general trends in fringe benefits and other employee advantages. These moves have all stood us in good stead when the question of the organizational labor unions has been raised. Our employees have appreciated the efforts we have made to be fair with them. They have been fair with us.

Another matter was constantly being called up for consideration over a long period of years before consensus could be reached. It dealt with the church grading system used for our educational organizations. While churches are at total liberty to build their own schedules and programs under our Baptist system of local church autonomy, they have found it highly advantageous to use the same basic grading system Convention-wide. When other denominations started grading according to school grades, the question was frequently raised with us about the plan for Southern Baptists.

There were fifty-eight identifiable grading systems in the United States. The question centered on which one was best for our churches to use. Even more basic was the fact that when churches grade according to school age, only a portion of the membership of any church are in school. This would mean that every church would have at least two grading systems—one for the ones in high school and below, and another grading system for those who had finished school. Obviously the pure school grading system could not apply to everyone.

Too, we discovered that the trend in public school was toward age group grading, which we were already using in our Sunday Schools and Church Training programs. When we conferred with the national

authorities about their future directions, it was suggested that we hold
the line and stay with the age group grading. They were coming
to us. Their experiments showed that the child who was promoted
each year with his own peer group despite academic achievements
was a better adjusted person with fewer hostilities than the ones who
were failed several times and ended up with resentments.

What we actually did was hold the line on age group grading until
the public school system moved far enough toward us to mesh the
two. Flexibility was built into the system also so churches could go
either way according to their desires. Appropriate literature would
be developed by us to meet any conceivable situation.

Having once developed the theory we went into consultation with
state leadership and other Convention agencies, testing situations in
local churches and experimenting in every way that we knew to
validate the system. Then we got it approved denomination-wide and
set the date for the transition. We conducted special training programs
so that people would be familiar with what we were doing and why.
We moved into the new system as smoothly as any massive readjustment could be made when covering a nation. The new grading
system has worked out beautifully. Churches have found merit in
it. Some have had to shift periodicals they were using. They found
some too complex, others too elementary. The system of curriculum
building had been developed to make such selectivity possible, so
it was merely a matter of adjusting up and down in the ordering
of periodicals until the correct ones were chosen for each given situation and each particular age group in each church. The new system
has been validated now by public acceptance, which has been enthusiastic. We felt it worth our while that we did hold to the age group
system until the present pattern of grading was possible. We made
it available to the people as soon as the situation seemed to warrant.

The growth of Southern Baptists and the Sunday School Board
raised other questions that we had to deal with because a number
of Southern Baptists had moved into western Canada. They began
to function as Southern Baptist churches, but that was outside the
territory of the United States and its possessions, which had been
the traditional area in which the Southern Baptist Convention had

functioned. It was also outside the area defined in our Convention's constitution and bylaws. It was felt that work in areas outside our nation should be done through mission boards, especially the Foreign Mission Board. Some practical polity problems were raised and policy questions were asked which were valid. It was finally determined by the Southern Baptist Convention in annual session that members of the Canadian churches, although they could cooperate as fully with state conventions as those state conventions wished and would allow, they as churches could not be considered qualified to send messengers to the Southern Baptist Convention churches because of their territorial location. By the same token their members were not eligible to be elected as trustees of Southern Baptist Convention boards and agencies.

Instead, another route was taken. That was the establishing of a joint committee representing Southern Baptists and Canadian Baptists to work on the problem. A liaison worker was chosen who was suitable to both. He would handle communications between the two Baptist bodies so that any help Canadians desired might be secured through regular channels. At the same time Canadians would not be threatened by an invasion by Southern Baptists, which some had felt was the case. There had been tensions developing toward Southern Baptists because many Canadians felt that territorial boundaries were not being respected in the direct work being done.

While the Southern Baptist Convention does work the world over, it is organized to do its work outside the United States through its Foreign Mission Board or through the Baptist World Alliance which is made up of Baptist bodies of all nations. While everyone is interested in the spread of the gospel everywhere, it seemed the route that Southern Baptists took was best. While the work has not progressed in Canada as fast and far as some Baptists there have wished, it still seems best for promotion and denominational work to be done there through the organized constituent Baptist body of that area rather than by relating the work directly to the Southern Baptist Convention.

Along with the expansion of the Southern Baptist Convention and the Sunday School Board, another problem emerged. It concerned the housing for the other Convention agencies rent free within the Sunday School Board building. The Executive Committee, along with several of the smaller agencies, had rightly felt that they could not establish their identity while located within the Sunday School Board's vast physical facilities. When we came to the point of having to expand our physical properties, therefore, we raised the question whether it would be best for us to offer to donate the Frost Building for this housing. It was our first structure built under Dr. Frost's leadership. We agreed to have it completely updated prior to transfer of title, or we would contribute an equivalent amount in cash for the smaller agencies to relocate in some other part of the city and build the type of building they needed if they wished to do that. It was determined that approximately one and one-fourth millions of dollars would be necessary for all the planned improvements and transfer to the Frost building to take place. The Sunday School Board made the offer of the renovated building or funds for a new building to the Southern Baptist Convention through its Executive Committee. The latter offer was accepted. The Executive Committee was given the responsibility of proceeding to erect a new building which is now called the Southern Baptist Convention Building at 460 James Robertson Parkway, some dozen blocks away from the Sunday School Board. This has proven to be a good arrangement for all concerned. It gives the other agencies the identity they deserve. It means that they do not have to adjust their schedule of holidays and work hours to ours. Other operational decisions which an institution like the Sunday School Board had to decide in the light of calendar, shipping schedule, and other factors does not now affect them. Previously, they had been victimized by schedules we were forced by circumstances to follow. Therefore they did not have the liberty of making their own choices as they should.

The growth of the Convention has brought about some traumatic experiences in an opposite manner which I had not anticipated. Shifts in population have brought pressures for Baptist Book Store establishments. Then the population would shift again, meaning that the situation would change. We would have to close down a book store in one community and establish one miles away or in another city if we were to be successful from a business point of view, as well as provide distribution efficiency.

Baptist Book Stores are under constant attack because no store can carry full inventory. Churches frequently order things that have to be back-ordered from the warehouse. Understandable complaints are frequent. But these complaints are nothing when compared to the laments and sad expression coming from a community when a book store must be closed down. It turns out to be one of the most traumatic of experiences, producing about as much bad public relations as anything the Sunday School Board has to do. But there have been certain times that we have been forced to do it rather than subsidize a store that was sometimes losing as much as $20,000 a year simply to keep it open when the population of the community has changed or the distribution patterns of the area could not make the store self-sustained. This difficulty led us to the position that a book store should not be begun except by approval by one full board of trustees. Even then they were started only after intensive study and in areas where the trend seemed to indicate that the store could be happily located for quite a number of years.

Because of the growth of Southern Baptists and the need for better understanding, we have invited youths to sit in our board meeting and participate fully in our Board discussions. These have usually numbered five or six. They have come from all sections of the United States. They have been young women as well as young men. They have sat in on committees, entered fully into the discussions, and have represented the viewpoints of youth. From them we have been able to read future trends in our denomination and make preparation for such in our planning processes. A system has been set up where we could select the most outstanding people in particular fields. We now choose those who are most faithful to their churches and most loyal in attendance to their church organizations. Therefore, we have people of interest rather than self-interest. They have done much to contribute to our denomination.

Earlier we mentioned the fact that growth in a denomination produces headaches as well as thrills, and we told how an institution of influence is under incessant attack simply because it has influence. The larger an institution gets the more the people generally become suspicious of it. The public looks on organization as impersonal and feels perfectly free to attack it whether justified or not. Well-chosen personnel is the best counteraction an institution like the Sunday School Board can take, and we have.

One of the most harrowing problems growing out of these years was related also to the racial strife and the forced school busing system in America. When a community was forced to integrate its school system, the whole community was understandably in upheaval. We have been able to pinpoint those areas of strife before the explosion has come by the nature of our letters from the territory involved.

Our publications did not back away from their historic stand that we should be Christian at all times to all races regardless of circumstances. While we never promoted integration per se, we always pushed for a Christian attitude toward all people. We took the position that all mankind is created in the image of God and made for a divine purpose. As Christians we can do no less than help each person find what the divine purpose for each life is and assist each person in achieving it. This position we have advocated and even defended vigorously. It is a positive approach. It calls for a Christian attitude toward all people at all times and the maintaining of a Christian relationship regardless of tensions which might exist in the nation or social structures about us at any given time.

We were somewhat perplexed, therefore, when public attacks were made against us in the form of written resolutions sent out by a certain community which was in upheaval. Letters were mailed to associational organizations all over the state begging them to take action condemning "Southern Baptist literature." They charged us with boldly promoting integration. Because we are the basic organization which produces Southern Baptist literature, the Baptist associations in that particular state apparently did not raise questions about any circumstances. The majority of them did take actions of condemnation against us. They mailed condemnations to us. It turned out that the church that had originated the appeal for condemning resolutions was actually referring to publications of two other Southern Baptist Convention agencies, not any of our publications. They were not a part of the Sunday School Board. Thinking that we were the ones who published these materials, they had taken their vigorous positions. We were the ones, therefore, who came under attack. We received noisy opposition about publications which were not even ours. We had not been related to them during development or distribution, but we received the criticism.

The church which originated the appeal for resolutions of condemnation against Southern Baptist literature to be drawn was horrified that they had made such a mistake, but the error had been committed. Flames of emotion had been fanned unintentionally. This explains in some measure the hostility the Sunday School Board experienced at the New Orleans Convention which came immediately thereafter. The resolutions of condemnation against the Sunday School Board had been distributed and discussed in virtually every association of that state which was not too many miles from New Orleans.

Growth has its problems as well as its glories. Difficulties in expansion should not cause the denomination to slow down or back away. Its efforts in growth must be constant because the words "all men," "everywhere," "ends of the earth," and "whosoever" are pivotal words in the New Testament. These words place binding obligations on us to do our sincere best to reach all men everywhere with the full gospel.

It is far better to live with the aggravating problems of youth than to suffer the stagnation of senility. Growing pains might have hurt, but they have been signs of health, not of disease.

# 6
# Role of Servant

In a very real sense my life has been given without reservation to areas that were service oriented, humanitarian in nature, and spiritual in impact. The mercenary side of life has concerned me very little. Never once did I ever negotiate for salary at any place where I ever worked. The institution for which I worked determined the salary. I accepted it as final and did the best I knew how to do, never counting costs or rewards. If they had reduced my salary 50 percent at any given time, I would have worked just as hard the next day without complaint and with no feeling that I was being discriminated against.

On one occasion I did receive a call from two churches on the same day. One of them offered me exactly twice the salary of the other. Although it might seem strange, I went to the church offering the lesser salary. I had a deep conviction that it was where the Lord wanted me. It turned out that this was the church that cast the direction of my future, teaching me more than I had learned anywhere else. Its years were some of the most difficult I have experienced, but that pastorate led me to see that God never leads one into a valley of shadows without keeping his promise to lead through that valley as well. The lesson of those years has helped me be ready for the intensity of responsibility and emotional drain involved in the type position I have held more than twenty years. Each of my pastorates proved to be a blessing in a different way.

During college days I had not accepted pastoral work although I had several opportunities. Being captain of the football team and president of the student body as well as director of the Training Union in the college church, I felt that my time was being occupied as fully as I could allow and in a way that would be profitable. Perhaps

I was learning more in these places than I would learn serving as a student pastor. Anyway those latter lessons could come in seminary days. My experiences in diversified campus responsibilities during college years, I felt, would broaden the base of my personal experience. They did.

Even though I had not accepted a pastorate during the Mississippi College days, I found that my going to that school was one of the wisest decisions I ever made. It is the oldest senior college of the state, rich in traditions and glorious in heritage. It somehow makes unique contributions to its students in lasting ways felt for a lifetime. It had a cluster of teachers committed to truth. They exemplified high ideals in many ways. In relationship with the students and in their ability in their fields, they could not have been surpassed.

I had been at the Southern Baptist Theological Seminary in Louisville only a short time when I received a request from the Mount Moriah Baptist Church in Boston, Kentucky. They asked if I would come down and help them some if my schedule allowed.

One of the oldest churches of the state founded in the latter 1700's, it was a small congregation in a little community a few miles south of Louisville. Because of train schedules I could commute easily, so I accepted. They had preaching services only once each month. I assisted them during my first year at the seminary as best I could, but it was with the understanding that if I had opportunity for a full-time work and felt that the Lord was leading in it that I would accept such when the opportunity arose.

A call to the Beaver Dam, Kentucky, Baptist Church came in a unique manner. Just as my first year at the seminary was closing, I was assisting Pastor Cecil Stephens at the Clifton Baptist Church in Louisville in his Vacation Bible School. I was staying in the city during the summer and not returning to Mississippi between sessions. Dr. Stephens had been reared in West Kentucky near Beaver Dam and still had a number of cousins in the area. It was rather natural when a crisis developed there that they would make contact with him. The pastor of the church, Brother C. C. Daves, had died of pneumonia a few months before. They had scheduled someone to come before the church with the view of considering him for a call.

He became sick Saturday night and could not fill his appointment. That meant they were without a preacher, and it was Saturday night— only a matter of hours until the worship service was scheduled. By telephone they were begging Brother Stephens desperately to send someone down. Since I was with him in the Vacation Bible School, it was natural that he turned to me. That trip was memorable. I thought it would be my first and last visit to this lovely little Kentucky community where I met some of the finest Baptist people I have ever met anywhere.

I caught the train down, arriving about midnight. Only two people were meeting the train. One was the depot agent and the other was the night watchman. When I asked the night watchman if he would direct me to a nearby hotel, he said: "I'll go with you across the way to a hotel since it's only a few hundred yards, but I'm afraid it is locked up. If it is, there is no way to get the owner to open up this late at night." Sure enough, we found ourselves locked out with nowhere to go for the rest of the night. Because my coming was rather sudden and there was no opportunity for prior planning I felt disadvantaged.

Finally in desperation to help the night watchman said: "I know of only one place for you to sleep. It's in a boarding house over a beer parlor." So as a last resort I let him direct me to this unwelcomed location. I got the one room available. The next morning I was awakened by rain falling in torrents. I was in a strange place, not knowing a person in town, and not knowing where the church was located. There was not even a telephone in my room.

I dressed and was standing at the foot of a long flight of stairs in a quandary when a green Dodge pulled up out front. The driver stuck his head out in the rain to say: "I'm looking for a Baptist preacher. Do you know where one is?" My response was: "I'm a Baptist preacher. Do you know where the Beaver Dam Baptist Church is?" In that strange manner we got together.

I found in this coal mining town a lovely brick building recently completed and debt free. I learned that the church had been there since the latter 1700's when it was founded by a group of the early pioneers. I enjoyed preaching to the people before returning to Louisville, never knowing that I would ever see them again.

When Morton Williams, the chairman of the deacons in Beaver Dam, telephoned me a few weeks later to tell me that I had been called as pastor of the Beaver Dam Baptist Church, I was only twenty-three years of age. I asked him if the call was unanimous. His response was, "No, it was not." Said he: "You got all but six votes, but George Truett wouldn't have gotten those either. He's been to school also." When I asked for an explanation, he told me that there were a half dozen retired preachers in the church, all of whom has lost their last pastorates to seminary trained men. While these men were quite different in attitudes, concepts, and temperaments and were in disagreement among themselves on many things, they all agreed on one fact—that the seminary was a threat to them. Its graduates were taking their places in the churches. All six of them had come to join the church in Beaver Dam. In unison they had argued that they were against "Sears and Roebuck preachers"—me included. They said they wanted God-called men, not man-made ones. Therefore, they worked against my coming. Even though they had made a house-to-house canvass to try to keep others in the church from voting for me the following day, they were the only six who did. Even their wives and children had supported my call.

Under those circumstances I accepted and went to Beaver Dam with the avowed purpose of making these six ex-pastors my best friends. I think I succeeded before each died, and five of my happiest years were spent there as undershepherd.

After a few trying but rewarding years in Ripley, Tennessee, which is more like a Mississippi River Delta town, I went back into the college town to pastor a church across from my alma mater in Clinton, Mississippi. I found this to be the church with the most rapid response, the largest attendance, and most challenging opportunity of any church I had served up to that time. Transportation for students over the weekend was unknown, so nearly the entire student body was in every service. This was true not only on Sunday but on Wednesday evenings as well. We preached to multitudes each time. There are people in Christian leadership all over the world now who were students there at the time. After I had been pastor there only a short while, World

War II broke out. Mississippi College was a boys' school, and we watched the virtual evacuation of the student body to all parts of the world in the war effort.

It was then that I went to Brookhaven (Mississippi) to be pastor of the First Baptist Church, one of the loveliest little Southern cities in which anyone could ever live. We found these profitable years also, although they were intense ones. We were there during World War II and had to tailor our ministry to meet the tragedies and griefs brought about by the loss of loved ones in the war struggle. We suffered shortages and rationing with the whole nation that time.

World War II had just ended when I came to the Belmont Heights Baptist Church in Nashville, Tennessee, as pastor. It was a church with a nationwide influence because a vast number of field workers of the Sunday School Board were members of that congregation. This gave me an understanding of the denomination that I treasure greatly. Also it taught me the value of having trained church members who can do their work with skill as well as understanding and who can be humble as well as knowledgeable.

Some of the struggling young businessmen of that congregation have now risen to the highest levels in American commerce and wealth. My prayer is that my influence with them then will continue in their massive decision-making processes that are worldwide in effect.

Abilene, Texas, my last pastorate, was different from the rest. The people were still pioneers in spirit. The church, founded the year the city was begun, held a unique place in West Texas. The building in which I preached when I arrived had been dedicated with the preaching of George W. Truett. Dr. Lee R. Scarborough had gone from that pastorate to head the evangelism department at South-western Seminary. Indeed the pastor of that church was accepted, sight unseen, as the No. 1 citizen of the city the day he arrived. The position was just that strategic.

Already having the rallying support of the people, we launched into a building program immediately in order to care for the tremen-dous weekly overflow of people. This resulted in the erection of one of the finest church structures in the Southern Baptist Convention. The First Church of Abilene comes as near being my ideal of a truly great church as any I know.

These years in the pastorate taught me how to love people, work with people, relate to organizations, plan objectives, deal with opposition, make difficult decisions, stand by those decisions even under stress, and still keep a good relationship with the masses so that no one would be personally offended by what we were seeking to do. This indeed is the role of the servant. I had been taught this by family tradition and pastoral experience.

Actually, the Sunday School Board came into existence to fulfill this same type role. Without this spirit it could not have served at all. Under Southern Baptist polity, the local church is the major organizational unit. It makes the final decision in everything, so the role of any denominational agency is never more than an influence, a suggestion, a recommendation, or an offer of assistance. There its power stops. It holds no control over any congregation or any Baptist. In such a situation one has to earn his right to influence by the quality and spirit of leadership and service given.

The Sunday School Board has developed many assets in the course of the years. It has grown from a borrowed corner in which it started to more than twenty acres of office space in the city of Nashville. This is in addition to more than fifty book stores in that many different, strategic cities. There are also Ridgecrest and Glorieta, two major conference centers in which something like 380,000 man-days of teaching and training are given in the course of a single year.

Under God, the Board has been able to secure the services of some of the most capable and dedicated workers of any denomination. They are willing to travel day and night and be away on the road at great sacrifice for prolonged periods to help the churches they can be and do a better job for Christ. Still the greatest asset of the Sunday School Board is the confidence the people have in it. As far as we have been able to determine, no other denominational publishing house has ever succeeded in distributing its educational materials to approximately 110 percent of its enrolment, with its recommended programs and projects practiced north, south, east, and west. This role of leadership has been earned through the servant relationship the institution has maintained. It has succeeded in keeping a proper relationship

to the churches. Churches are not threatened by it but are appreciative
of its influence, the validity of its recommendations, and the simplicity
of its processes.

Perhaps if I had been a pushy type of person and had assumed
the autocratic role of a hard driver pushing toward more accomplishments in enrolment and enlistment, we could have had more people
on the rolls of the Sunday Schools of the Southern Baptist Convention.
It would have been possible with a concerted effort and intense
promotion. My conviction is, however, that sustained growth does
not come through that type of program. Fellowship is one of the
greatest possessions a church has. Programs should be developed and
promoted in such a way that the people can enthusiastically support
them on an ongoing basis out of conviction. Such requires time. Never
should promotion get ahead of education, or there will be a backlash
which can prove costly. So we have tried to pace the development
and promotion of programs at the Sunday School Board in such a
way that the churches would be strengthened on a permanent basis
so there would be no later regrets. Every program has been planned
with the local church in mind. When the final decisions were made,
they were all made with the view of producing lasting good and
constant growth. Only with the attitude of a servant and a relationship
of helpfulness can this be attained and maintained.

The course we have followed has been one of philosophy and we
have felt that it is the right one. Under our polity any church can
veto any decision made by the Board or denomination. If we ever
move too fast or too far, or veer to the right or to the left unduly,
churches that wish to do so can reject our materials, refuse our programs, and move in any direction they choose. We have no recourse.
When such happens, school is out for us. We have lost our opportunity
to serve them ever unless of their own volition they choose to return
to the use of our materials. We defend this principle and have a
deep conviction concerning this polity, so we support this type of
inter-relationship. We defend this power of veto on the part of the
local congregations. While it creates problems from time to time, on
the whole it is the safest position we can take or follow. It keeps
us on the alert, makes us produce not only the finest of commodities

but also recommend the most effective and practical of programs.

Because of the nature of our denomination and the Sunday School Board in the servant role, a great deal of time must be spent in prayer and questing for the leadership of the Holy Spirit. In this way we can be assured that the work we do is lasting as well as acceptable. This approach recognizes the spiritual nature and impact of the institution. It must be consciously spiritual in every plan and must keep before its workers the spiritual nature of the institution and the spiritual impact it is having upon the people and the nation. Never can the Sunday School Board follow a rigid role of a strict business operation, giving attention only to cold organizational principles, methodology, or finances. These are important, but the really important thing is the ultimate spiritual impact. The work we do affects spiritual lives and homes of the people whom we serve by the millions. We insist that a great deal of time be spent in prayer questing for the leadership of God's spirit. With his leading in our planning processes and leading the churches in their adopting and promotion of the programs, we will be moving together. If we are both led by the same divine power and motivated by the same divine wisdom we will walk together as brethren.

There are those who think that the Sunday School Board's programs are planned by people sitting at a desk far removed from the churches. When they have this concept, they totally misunderstand what happens. It is true that programs are projected in our publications and that there are many decisions which we do make. But they are made in the framework of guidelines given us by the Convention. Furthermore, they are made with the help of others and in consultation with representatives from the various state conventions, associational organizations, Baptist institutions, and other Convention agencies. Pastors of local churches, workers with varying age groups, representatives of geographical areas of our Convention, and others who can contribute to the development of sound practical programs to help the churches do what the New Testament has asked them to accomplish are asked to participate. Even then the programs offered are approved by the Convention in broad guidelines. The emphases are promoted simultaneously by all agencies after emerging through grass roots development and planning. They are not programs that are handed down. They are programs that are developed by mutual participation of Baptists at all levels of organization and in all areas of denominational life. While the process is slow, it is by far the best system we have been able to devise and has proved to be practical as well.

One of the problems the Sunday School Board faces that the average Baptist seldom is aware of concerns caused by geographical differences of people who occupy the United States. The Sunday School Board produces materials for churches in all fifty states. In doing so we become painfully aware of geographical differences. We have to find ways of taking out a writer's provincialisms that can be misunderstood. We must communicate in such a way that people will not get different ideas from the same words in our published materials. It is not easy to produce materials that serve a metropolitan downtown church like the First Baptist Church of Dallas which covers three city blocks and is located in the shadow of skyscrapers on land so expensive it is bought by the square foot, and have those same materials communicate in the same effective way to some church up a cove in the coal fields of some mining camp in the mountains. People are so isolated there that they seldom see people from other parts of the world unless they have come in for some specialized ministry. Preparing materials which will be usable by new and old churches or by churches of any age, nature, and location has been one of our objectives. We seek to defend the diversity of our churches feeling that in this manner we can be of best service to them and Baptists can be better Baptists.

Illustration of the broad reach of the Board came when I found myself at Glorieta seated by one of the most interesting characters I have ever met. He was a heavyset mountaineer, of ruddy complexion. He had on a sport shirt with short sleeves, but he was so engrossed in everything said and done that I was impressed by him. He functioned like a blotter soaking up ink. He was taking in everything that was said in most enthusiastic fashion.

As soon as adjournment came, I turned to him with the question, "Have you ever been to Glorieta before?" His response was that he had not. Then he proceeded to say that it is the most wonderful experience of his life. "I'm grateful for the opportunity of being here. It's absolutely glorious." When I asked him the circumstances under which he came, he explained that his church back home needed a new building. Since he was superintendent of Sunday School at the time, they had made him chairman of the committee to plan such a structure. Not knowing what to do, he had written the Sunday School Board in Nashville to secure suggestions. They sent blueprints that they thought might meet their needs. One of the plans was exactly what the church was looking for. The church approved the plans sent from the Sunday School Board. Then they named the same man chairman of the building committee. Thus he had supervised the construction. He said, "When we competed the building, the people were so happy that they contributed enough money for us to pay the total cost of the building. Then they took up an offering to send me to Glorieta. My coming is an expression of their appreciation for my long hours given, both in planning and in leading the building program for our church." He concluded: "The most glorious thing about it is, I am a dairyman, and they're milking my cows while I'm gone."

This incident merely points up that there is no place in the land and not many countries of the world where literature and programs of the Sunday School Board are not found. Capable and dedicated planners and writers put much of themselves into the processes of development. The materials produced will apply most anywhere and with God's help the influence of it has been tremendous. The acceptance of the Sunday School Board's materials and programs have been the envy of other denominations, who while they have much closer denominational controls on their churches and congregations, have never been able to match the support and confidence Baptists have given the Sunday School Board throughout its history.

Maintaining this servant role is exhausting, but the Board has no alternative. Many times I have traveled ten or twelve thousand miles in a month's time covering various part of the country in every conceivable type of situation to try to find out what the churches are like. I needed to know what they needed, what they wanted, what they were thinking, and where we were failing to meet their needs.

I needed to discover what the future directions should be, how we could do better planning in the course of the future, and where there might be additional writers who could help us prepare the multitudinous materials in an even better way.

Something like eighteen hundred writers are required in a year's time to produce the educational materials needed in the furtherance of our work. We have a great variety and diversity of penmen. They give endless hours each month to the preparation of manuscripts meeting the needs of churches in a particular way. They live all over the nation. They are members of the churches who live on the field and they know Baptists firsthand.

One of the problems we face is finding enough committed writers who are willing to spend the time necessary in the preparation of manuscripts. Writing is a discipline. It calls for hard work and regular study. Not every person is able to concentrate in that manner or find time in the schedule for the purpose of doing it even when they're capable as scholars and have time on their hands to write. Not every one has the incentive to do it. Even then they might not have the writing skills that will enable them to communicate properly with the pen. Writing demands a multiplicity of talents. Too, it perhaps demands as much patience as any profession a person can follow. Nevertheless, we have found our writers from the pastorate, professorships, and various professions. They come from church staffs. They are housewives. They are laymen who are either at work or retired. Each has a particular gift. All are willing to serve God and to help meet Baptist needs.

The Sunday School Board must keep abreast in its public relations. Therefore we give a great deal of attention to the letters we receive. They are expressive of attitudes not only of different geographical areas but of different types of churches. We tabulate these, analyze them, and take them into account in future planning. We never ignore or disregard any, regardless of source. Usually we can tell at a glance whether the letter is sincere and the criticism justified, or whether there is a local situation which someone is resenting or resisting and he is having to vent his emotions on us. We never fight back. Some of the letters are obviously the writings of extremists. Others are from irrational people who offer ridiculous ideas and impractical proposals. The great majority of them however come from sincere, conscientious people. They are expressing their honest judgments in simple words and are trying to help us do our work in a better way. Therefore, they have every right to be heard. Their suggestions are given every consideration.

I think everyone should understand that we tend to give more attention to a handwritten letter than we will one typed. This is because it is easy for a man to sit down at a dictating machine or before a private secretary and vent his emotions orally. It takes a lot more time, patience, and effort for a person to write his explanation or suggestion in a letter written in long hand. Our experience has been that a person is ten times more apt to criticize than compliment. Therefore, if we get one hundred criticisms and ten compliments about the same act or publication, we know the opinion is fifty-fifty.

Because of the servant role of the Board and the people who work for the institution, it is amazing the high respect people generally have for Sunday School Board employees. This is a thing that we do not seek. Only when something unusual occurs do we think about it at all. Traveling from place to place all hours of the day and night, it is nothing for a ticket agent at a counter or a clerk in a hotel, or a driver of a bus, even a pilot of a plane to recognize who you are and to comment about the denomination and the institution for which you work. They hold the employees of the Sunday School Board in high regard because the institution has been cautious in employment, setting high standards of morality and efficiency for its people. This has built a relationship to the general public which would be the envy of any ordinary business concern. It is doubtful that a business anywhere engaged in an operation for the making of money could ever have the heart-to-heart relationship of the populace that an institution like the Sunday School Board has. It exists to render a service and to fulfil its spiritual mission in a servant role.

One of the incidents that points up the respect held for the institution and the people who work there came in a West Texas town where I had gone to speak. That morning my alarm clock failed to go off. Discovering that it was not functioning, I decided to take it by a little watch shop I had seen nearby to have the watchmaker check it out. It was a clock which was given to me as a Christmas gift by the William Hall Prestons when I was their pastor. My name was embossed in gold on the back. It was a folding travel clock, and I had used it long and to great advantage.

When I took the clock to the watchmaker, he saw the name embossed on the back, and said, "I don't want to fix this clock, but I'll trade it." In surprise I asked him what he meant. He said, "Are you the man with the name on the back of this clock?" I answered in the affirmative. Then he continued, "I'll tell you what I'll do. I'll give you a brand new travel clock if you'll trade me this old one." When I asked him, "What's up?" he said: "I am a Baptist. I've known of you since I was a boy. I have read your writings year after year with appreciation. I would count it a privilege to have this clock for my personal possession, and I'll give you a brand new one if you'll let me have this old one you've used these years. I will count it a personal treasure."

I was utterly amazed at his attitude as well as the generosity of his offer. I, of course, took him up on it partially. I gave him the old one but bought and paid for a new one. I went away shaking my head, thinking how easily I could have gone into that store in an ill-tempered manner, acting unchristian in attitude and conduct. I would have reflected on the institution without ever knowing that the person there to whom I was talking knew virtually everything about me although I had never seen him before and did not even know who he was. This experience points up the fact that Sunday School Board workers are under constant surveillance by watchful eyes of Southern Baptists the nation over. They know who our people are. At times they put us to personal tests just to see if we practice what we teach and preach. We're happy that our employees do measure up almost without exception, although all of us are still painfully human in our own eyes.

# 7
# Learning Through Trials

We have dealt briefly with some of the difficulties we have faced. Each taught us lessons. Some of the most valuable lessons, however, were learned through observation and analysis during day-to-day operations.

There is no more accurate indicator of how things are moving in the churches than how the Sunday School Board is doing. When the churches grow and advance, the requests for additional literature are received immediately. When the churches are in trouble, the Sunday School Board has troubles, and immediately. What's more, we sometimes experience trouble before the churches do, because a part of our role is to protect the churches. The enemies of Christianity cannot well get at the churches unless they lash out at us and weaken us first.

The past two decades have been rapidly expanding years, and expansion brings peculiar problems all its own as we have already shown. Expanding buildings, additional personnel, more complicated processes, greater expenditures and a host of other headaches, all accompany growth. While they are headaches of a good kind, they still demand much time and heavy outlay of expense as well as readjustment and balance in organization. During these twenty-one years, the growth of the Board has been phenomenal, indicating the continuing good health of the churches. The annual budget in the Board's operation when I assumed office was nearly $16,000,000. During my last year in office the Board's budget was approximately $60,000,000. While some was due to inflation, the major portion was due to expansion in every area of the Board's life. And when growth in any institution exceeds 10 percent a year, the chief administrator feels that he is fighting a brush fire just to stay ahead of things.

Some of the most valuable lessons we have learned have issued from the growth of the Board and the Convention it serves. Some of the major lessons of these years are:

1. There is no such thing as progress without opposition. It is much like a football game where each runner must expect a potential tackler. Each year of advance has to be brought about by a planned strategy and intensive effort. Or, life is like an automobile building up wind pressure as it increases its speed. The faster it goes, the more powerful the wind resistance against it. This principle is inherent in the very nature of progress itself. While this principle applies in the mechanical and business realms, as the heads of corporations know, it is all the more true in religion, where the devil enters the fray to throw obstacles in the way of progress. He wants to lessen spiritual impact.

While this principle applies all the time, there are certain seasons when rebellion is intensified. The 1960's proved to be just that sort of decade. Rebellion was upon us. Very few people in roles of leadership knew why, but all were experiencing difficult situations simultaneously especially if they were related to institutions of influence. They were considered a part of "the establishment." While college presidents perhaps caught things the hardest, no one in a role of responsibility was far behind. During that decade it seemed that some people would go out of their way to embarrass or heckle. An illustration was the college boy who kept parking his car in the parking spot bearing my name. He paid no attention to instruction to park elsewhere. In my in-and-out work, I would drive back to find my spot taken. When I got stern and ordered him away with the threat of arrest, he returned to chop down the tree under which I had parked and stole the "No Parking" sign which he had been disregarding. During that decade of rebellion we had bomb threats. There was attempted industrial sabotage. There were other planned interruptions. Articles appeared in magazines and papers attacking us for not opening our doors wide to everybody and inviting people into our building, even if they were planning to steal purses and coats from employees or merchandise from our storeroom while there. In our downtown area, drunks would roam aimlessly about the buildings. Employees were threatened. When we put in a security system, the

howls grew loud. Interestingly enough, many attacks were traceable
to students who felt we were too slow in crusading for social progress.

2. World situations demand changes in approaches. This should
be apparent but it is not an easy thing to adjust to. Change is difficult
by its very nature. When there is a shifting scene in a world situation,
an institution like the Sunday School Board can be thrown into
traumatic experiences of readjustment as its seeks to communicate
and serve. Change is always difficult. One of the memorable pranks
we pulled in college days was to go into a student's room while he
was in class, take his furniture out of his room, and put it in a vacant
room nearby. When he would come back from class, he would be
totally lost. The experience was not only disconcerting, it would almost
blow the mind as he tried to figure out what had happened to him.
If changing visible things like this can create emotional strains, it
is understandable how much truer it is in the educational field or
as one works in the spiritual realm where things are largely invisible
but are just as genuine and far more lasting.

Language, for instance, is constantly changing. The meanings of
words not only are altered but sometimes reverse themselves. Unless
we take this into account and do our writing and editing accordingly,
we are apt to miscommunicate or even offend people. Who would
have thought a few years ago that the word "streaking" would take
on its present meaning? We will be saying something that is entirely
different from what those same words might have meant even one
year before if we're not careful.

There has been the organizational pattern recommended for departments and classes in a different grading system. Formats for publications change. These are updated periodically because of technical
changes in printing processes, but there are people who have difficulty
understanding why.

Certain things we do seem strange to the outsider. When facts about
what we do are known, things can take on different meanings. An
illustration deals with former mailings of book store catalogs. Frequently pastors received two copies. We always got letters asking why
we were so wasteful and extravagant by letting two copies be sent
to the same person. On the surface this did seem extravagant and

seems a logical criticism. The fact is we have kept up more than one hundred separate mailing lists simultaneously at the Board. To go through all of these lists with tens of thousands of names to remove the duplicates would have cost several times more than the few extra catalogs would cost. Therefore, we found it to be a matter of economy even though it appears to be an extravagance. When the world gets into a period of war, depression, inflation, permissiveness, or legalism, each will have an effect on the way the Sunday School Board functions. The mind set of the people is influenced by changing situations. We must be aware of this even if they are not.

3. People on the whole are basically honest and sincere. If someone is dishonest or insincere, or meets some that way, he tends to wonder if all humanity is not that way. Especially is this true if one has had a traumatic experience accompanied by emotion or resentment. All of us tend to universalize our experiences. If one person proves to be dishonest, it is easy to assume that all people are. If we begin acting out of prejudice and blind emotion, however, such error takes its toll on us for not making a right distinction.

We do have to deal with some people who are dishonest because we operate in the area of manufacturing, buying, selling, and interpersonal relationships. These, however, are in the extreme minority. The thing that causes me to marvel is that there are so many good people in the world with high ethical standards and high moral practices. They are totally honest in their dealings and sincere in every human relationship. Even they, however, need the gospel. So the church in its work does not find a lesser job to do after it has won people to Christ. There is a lifetime of instruction to follow in order that one might reach his highest potential in Christian achievement and motivation, even if he is a good person by the world's standards.

4. Our Baptist way is slow and expensive, but it is still the best. Each denomination has its own approach. Some follow a purely totalitarian system with a hierarchical structure. Such is by far the most economical and efficient. There is nothing to do except pass an order down and receive a report back. The processes can be speedy, the method efficient, and the system effective. Baptists, however, have rejected such a hierarchical approach in our denomination because

of what it does to the individuals involved. Down the ladder of the hierarchy personal liberties tend to erode and be lost. The competency of the soul is overlooked, and decisions are made at higher levels without explanation or even consideration for the rights of all people involved.

Operating somewhat like a courtroom where processes must be slow because human rights are at stake, Baptists have chosen deliberative processes. We try to make decisions after depth discussions. The best judgment of the group is discovered and followed. This process is not only slow, it is costly. For instance, many man-hours are involved due to the massive attendance at Conventions. History has proved, however, the necessity of our operating in this manner. Even though processes are slow and the costs high, it is the only way a grass roots denomination like ours can keep abreast of the times and meet the needs of the churches as they seek to bring God's will to pass. The more I have seen our Baptist processes and procedures, the deeper my convictions are that we have the best system of any major denomination. It is built more according to the pattern of the New Testament than any other known approach and it works.

5. When one acts in a crisis, he tends to overact. This is what makes a crisis a very crucial time. One not only recognizes an acute problem, but in his solution of it, he can unwittingly create another problem bigger than the first. Especially is this true if one acts without proper analysis, makes decisions under pressure, or feels that the solution of one problem will make all the difficulties go away. One of the first things a person learns in administration is that all problems can never be removed. Frequently, the solution of one problem creates other problems, we hope of a lesser kind and more bearable. There's no such thing as a perfect system, and problems do not go away entirely even when a solution appears. Problems merely appear in different forms. This principle was called to my attention by Dr. Rupert Richardson, president of Hardin-Simmons University, when he retired from his post. He told me something that has been invaluable to me in the course of my years: "Administration is like building a house with warped boards. You nail one end down and the other end flops loose. You run to the far side to nail that one down, and the first

end begins to flop." He said: "I've been president of the university for ten years, have never gotten the board nailed down totally a day that I have been there. Half the time it was flopping at both ends." By these words he gave one of the best descriptions of the tentative nature of administration I have ever heard, pointing up the fact that there is no such thing as getting decisions nailed down so they will stay.

Institutions are living things. An administrator deals with constant movements which mesh together in awkward fashions. This in itself is difficult. It is oftentimes like handling a boat going down stream through rapids. While trying to keep the boat parallel to the bank and avoiding snags, you must maintain balance or you will capsize. You must take your actions according to precise timing and without fear or problems will compound quickly and become acute instantaneously.

6. People must have liberty of action within a framework of broad guidelines. Team play is impossible unless the players on a team know what they're to do, when and how, and the manner in which they are to relate to the other people on the team. An institution has to have a great number of creative people working for it if it is to be dynamic. Especially is this true when it has educational and promotional responsibilities like the Sunday School Board. But if the institution takes an autocratic attitude and demands that everyone say and do certain things in certain ways, the individual involved becomes unable to put himself and his personality into the project. He does a much lesser job as a result.

Our mode of operation across these years has been to use people who can promote the program of work in cooperation with their counterparts in state conventions, associations, and local churches. They would make recommendations jointly concerning actions seeming appropriate. We would examine their suggestions to see how their conclusions and recommendations fitted into the overall plan of the denomination. If all seemed to move together toward the objective we had in mind, if we were able to budget it, and if it did not create problems for others, we would put our signature to the project to authorize it. Then we would support it wholeheartedly.

One finds early that when one serves Baptists he cannot sit at a desk far removed from a local situation and plan a program diversified and practical enough to suit them. So we have never undertaken that method of planning.

Throughout our history we have leaned heavily upon the field persons who have responsibility of doing a job where the people are. We call meetings of representatives from over the nation to make a study and offer recommendations for our consideration. We simply refine their proposals, correlate them, validate them by necessary board and Convention authorization, and everything is on its way. Through this means, we have developed a denomination which follows the middle of the road of our broad constituency and provides practical materials and programs which the people have believed in and supported.

7. Maintaining balance is one of the most difficult arts. Administering an operation or organization is not too different in nature from a person standing at the fulcrum of a seesaw keeping balance. Have you ever watched youths on a seesaw? Each is trying to maneuver the seesaw so that he will be in control of the person at the other end of it. This is a game children play. All of us around school playgrounds have watched a person standing on that seesaw, placing one foot on each side of the fulcrum. The one standing at the fulcrum tries to maintain balance so that neither person will totally win or lose but each can ride high and be happy. It is the art of maintaining balance that makes the administrative load both difficult and endless.

Of course, there are some extremist organizations giving attention only to one side. They try to be devastating to their opposites or to any person who seeks to maintain balance. The Sunday School Board by its nature serves as a balance wheel of the denomination. Extremism comes into play frequently. A first move generally is an attack against this balancing task. An extremist does not want balance any more than he wants those with opposing views to win. His purpose is complete annihilation of the opposition. Too, he tends to consider a person seeking to maintain balance as a compromiser. Therefore, he puts him under assault as well as the opposition. Herein we suffer.

One of the dilemmas is that a person who is an extreme rightist naturally considers everybody to his left a modernist. A person who is progressive, even though not a modernist, tends to consider everybody right of him to be a fundamentalist with a capital *F*. This inevitable tension is apt to put a mediator or an administrator under attack from both sides simultaneously. It is the most difficult position of all.

Because of our responsibilities at the Sunday School Board, we've tried to stay alert to the situation at any given time. We have been thrust into the responsibility of maintaining balance, oftentimes working for sedimentation in the denomination and against agitation. We have been attacked by both the leftists and the rightists, but we've had no other option open to us if we were to fulfil our true function.

Someone has said that the only place an institution like ours can function is in the middle, but one can never afford to get caught there. Actually, however, we have analyzed all of our correspondence from constituents, and when all our criticisms are from one side, we reassess our position. It likely means we have unconsciously veered or else the world situation has changed. We need to take another bearing of position to see if we have unconsciously altered courses while we were preoccupied in other urgent matters.

This constant reassessment and reevaluation is necessary in the advance of the institution like ours, but it calls for the constant exercise of personal judgments. There is no instrument that is foolproof in providing all the information needed. This means that an administrator has to be rough and tough at times. It also means that he has to be exceedingly sensitive to existing circumstances, to people, to emotions, and to the temperament of the churches at any given time. How many times the words of my father have come back to me: "Son, you are more apt to get bitten by a snake when you are running from a bull than any other time. So always watch both ways." Indeed, danger is on both sides.

8. Team action is much better than individual approaches. It is difficult for some people to understand the necessity for teamplay in an institution like the Sunday School Board. We have no other course if we are to do the job assigned us. In athletics there are some games played individually like boxing. A boxer is on his own. He

does not have to relate to anybody or trust anybody. He has only his opposition to keep in mind. He makes his quick decisions and operates without consultation. He by himself either wins or loses.

A football team is exactly the opposite. Eleven men are on the field constituting that team. If one man loses the game, the whole team has lost. If one man succeeds, the whole team is successful. This is why they call signals, hold constant consultations, get evaluations from the other players, and invite suggestions concerning weak points in the line of the opposition. They operate in a concerted, coordinated fashion in a line drive or a forward pass.

The first thing a person learns in football is that there is no such thing as a one-man team. One man may conceivably be more outstanding than the others, but there's no such thing as one player being a team all to himself. Each position on the team calls for a certain type of player who functions in a particular manner. Some are not only eligible to do certain things but are trained especially for specific activities. A punter becomes a specialist in his area of punting, a passer becomes a specialist in the area of passing, or a runner becomes a specialist in the art of running, so each player has his own specialty in which he majors. Still his actions have to be coordinated with those of the blockers, tacklers, catcher of the passes, et cetera. While teamplay is desirable on a team or in a church, it is absolutely indispensable in an institution like the Board.

9. Communications is our most difficult problem. For a publishing house to have difficulty in communications may sound ironic. We reach millions of persons directly each week. We spend a considerable time trying to get ideas across. Where there are complexities of programming and a multiplicity of publications, it takes a long time for people to see the system and the science of what you're undertaking, yet they must if they are to get behind the movement in an organized, systematized, aggressive way. As someone has put it, it takes a long time to even say hello to Southern Baptists. This is true because of the geographical spread and the remoteness of many of the churches which makes communications all too inadequate at best. Long-range planning becomes a necessity because of this difficulty of communication. Plans have to be projected far in advance. This

makes planning hard. Just as the buyer in a department store finds it difficult to buy Christmas goods before Easter, or an artist finds designing a magazine for Easter difficult before Thanksgiving, so there is inherent difficulty in planning programs and projects so far in advance of the time of their appearance.

A few years ago, all the agency heads of Southern Baptist Convention agencies, boards, and institutions met with all the state executive secretaries at the Kentucky assembly to help lay plans and develop directions and programs to be considered by the Convention through the year 1979. It was called to the attention of that host of denominational workers that among the executive officers and presidents of the Convention agencies that only a couple of them would still be in office in 1979. Still it was necessary to do planning and definite work that far in advance. Programs must be refined by consultations with all of the areas of Baptist life, worked into publishing schedules, approved by Convention processes, and promoted by field workers in some twelve hundred associations and nearly thirty-five thousand churches if they are to be effective!

This difficulty in communications forces conscientious efforts at simplification both in program and materials. This is not an easy ideal or process. With purposeful effort we seek to simplify both program and project so that the average person in the average church can see it and take hold of it. He must see how it can benefit him where he is and how to apply the facts to his situation. This simplified and unified way of promotion through long-range planning has become a system necessary to us even though there are many difficult steps along the way.

To complicate the matter even more the Convention agencies have to do much joint planning because of complex interrelationships they have in program assignments. These must be harmonized. Nevertheless, the system works beautifully. When all work together, the accomplishments write history and produce achievements of which all are proud.

10. Keeping eyes on the ultimate goals is imperative. Before there can be accomplishments, objectives must be set. While these do not become ironclad laws, they establish the sense of direction for all

the employees of our institution and for the Convention which owns and operates us. This is what keeps an institution like ours from losing its bearings in a crisis and prevents workers of all levels of the Board's life from operating in a tug-of-war in which efforts and energies are spent in opposite directions.

These goals may be announced in a formal way with definite timetables set, or they may be more informal existing in the minds of the leadership. There are certain advantages in each approach, but always goals must be set within the overall purposes of the Convention. What the institution wishes to achieve through its activities must be kept in mind. Once an institution starts moving toward its objectives, the timetable may be altered to some degree in the light of existing circumstances. Tactics may be shifted periodically in the light of changing needs, but the ultimate goal remains the same regardless of changing scenes.

An administrator operates an institution while keeping in mind the definite things he is trying to accomplish. He exercises judgment along the route. His discussions are affected by situations and circumstances which may or may not have been anticipated.

The important thing is that the goal does not change. Strategies, tactics, and timetables may be altered in the light of unexpected or developing situations. Goals are never changed.

11. There is peril in operating in the middle. Southern Baptists have never been an extremist religious body. Any democracy is going to have a great deal of extremism. Extremists while bothersome can be of benefit to the democratic process. They can make the leadership more cautious in its activity, more thoughtful in the details of planning, and more efficient in the work done. It actually takes some degree of extremism to get people to apply themselves to certain problems in sufficient manner to get something done about it. Extremists render this service even if it is the uniting of our forces to withstand some extremism which appears to be getting out of hand. Sometimes it actually does. The subsequent injury for a time may be painful, yet even that experience can be therapeutic for the overall work of the Convention. It moves forward with greater speed than ever because the people must now address themselves to a common problem in

a united way. Such unity speeds up the progress of a democratic body.

Imagine the United States trying to come into nationhood without some extremists. They could not have done it. Admittedly, Patrick Henry was an extremist. From what is said about him, he must have been a rather difficult person to get along with. He was very opinionated and was free to express his opinions. He was bombastic in nature. He was indeed a fanatic. Had it not been for Patrick Henry's extremism, however, it is doubtful that the colonies would have ever been moved to the necessary point where united action was possible for the freedom of the country. Extremism of people like Patrick Henry moved the great silent middle to active concern and concerted effort.

One of the difficulties is that extremism of one kind tends to produce extremism of another kind at the opposite end of the spectrum. There is the cross-fertilization of ideas, the extended debates between the two groups, and final decision by the full body. Hopefully all will accept and practice things according to the majority once the vote is taken through democratic processes. They usually do.

When extremists get an extreme movement going, their first effort is to try to push institutions along with them in their upsurging movement. While institutions may have a slight degree of mobility, they can never swing with the crowds to an extreme position without falling apart. They have some degree of tolerance, but not that much.

Circumstances in which we live create movements much like the pendulum of a clock. Movements are in an alternated way from extreme leftists to extreme rightists. Governments change their leadership in the same way. So do institutions. The fact of the matter, however, is that almost without exception all administrators have to move to the middle of their constituency before they can function effectively. This puts all of them essentially in the same position with slight variations either right or left.

The disconcerting thing is that when there is an extreme swing—let it be fundamentalism or progressivism, let it be integration or segregation, or some other emotional cause—there are those who will feel that the current swing, whatever it is, is "the wave of the future." They climb aboard thinking that they are at the cutting edge of advance. What they discover later is that the motion they felt was only a pendulum swing. It was not the cutting edge. If an institution follows the course of extreme swings with the crowd, it will be left stranded in the vacuum when the backswing comes. And that backswing will come in due time and will be devastating.

The perennial rhythm in which an administrative officer lives keeps him watching these extreme swings passing through the body of the institutions he directs. First it is going in one direction, then in the opposite. These swings touch every part of the institution at the same time, and he must be alert to their influence and exercise judgment. Finally he has to say that this point is as far as the institution can go now. He nails it down there and says, "no further." Then he must ride out the storm regardless of intensity. If he doesn't protect the institution at this juncture, it flings apart, and the administrator has faltered when he was needed most.

This means that the administrative officer is under constant attack by both extremists at both ends of the line and all the time. It is a very uncomfortable position, but it is where he inevitably lives. If he is not willing to pay the price of making hard decisions for the purposes of maintaining balance in the organization of which he has been given leadership, he does not deserve the office to which he had been elected.

12. Even your nearest workers cannot always understand. I have been fascinated by the study of Christ's experience in Gethsemane. He would move with his disciples to try to gain comforting words from them only to find that they were asleep. If they weren't, they did not know what to say or how to say it. Then he would go back into the silence of the garden in prayer once more to spend time in meditation and prayerfulness alone. He would soon return again to his disciples to find them sleeping once more. He would know that even though they were close to him they could not understand the depth of his feeling or the nature of the problems with which he was wrestling.

Every administrative officer, if he is worth his salt, has his Gethsemane experiences. He alone must make certain decisions. No one else can make or even understand why they are made. He may be the president of the nation, the governor of a state, the chief justice of the Supreme Court, the pastor of a church, or the head of a denominational agency, but these moments come for all people in positions of responsible leadership. Agony of soul is experienced in an indescribable way. Emotions run deep. Decisions are of utmost importance. You and you alone must determine what that decision is to be. This is what produced the phrase "the loneliness of leadership."

This struck me rather dramatically when I had scheduled a number of statewide meetings that called for an unusual amount of cross-country travel. After the schedules had taken final form, airlines changed flight schedules. I found that I had to spend two of the nights of one week sitting up in planes most of the night going from one speaking engagement to another. That was bad enough. The problem was compounded when I learned that the state of Oregon had placed a tax assessment on the entire nationwide operation of the Sunday School Board nationwide simply because we were operating a small book store in Portland and even though we were subsidizing it some $20,000 a year just to keep it alive.

This meant that I had to go to Oregon that same busy week. I sat up one night going, spent the day in argument before the Tax Commission, and then returned the following night. With the state convention already scheduled, I had four consecutive nights of airplane travel. It was murderous. To add to the difficulty there was a very important meeting in Nashville which I had to attend immediately after my fourth night in planes. Upon arrival in Nashville I was hurrying from the airport to make the 10:30 morning meeting. Every joint in my body was aching because I had reached that point of sheer animal exhaustion because of the strain of so many consecutive overnight trips.

As I stepped on the elevator at the Board about 10:25, one of the secretaries stepped on at the same moment. Seeing my briefcase in my hand, she said, "I wish I were the boss of the institution so I could sleep late and come to work just any old time." I did not have the nerve to tell her the facts of the case. I knew she could never comprehend the burden of an executive officer, so I did not even bother to comment.

13. Never bend to pressure. Unless one has experienced it, he cannot realize the pressures some people and organizations can put on a chief executive officer in an effort to coerce him to bend an institution according to their individual liking. They usually pick or create a crisis time for their build-up of pressure. Methods they use are unbelievable. Usually they will launch an attack against the institution. Then they will organize people of like mind to make telephone calls either to you or your family in a systematic way by day and by night. They will send letters in great number, or have them sent. They will file requests with the government to check your personal income tax records, or without grounds they will file labor citations or post citations against you on government forms of undue length with the hope that you'll be completely occupied and cannot give yourself to the problem they are creating. In this way they hope to win by default. They will seek to block an institution in some of its most necessary activities unless there is yielding to their demands. It takes a person of stability to maintain equilibrium when such pressures are on with rapidity and intensity.

One can never afford to bend to the pressure extremists build up or yield to it to any degree.

I have often contended that if a leader ever adjusts to the lies told on him during a crisis created by a pressure group, that liars will then be in control of the institution. For this reason I never bent under pressure. To do so would only invite more pressure next time. While one must stay sensitive of the attitudes of all the people regardless of positions they hold, he must make his decisions on the basis of good judgment and sound planning. He must have a philosophy and operate out of it. Then he can ride out whatever storm may occur with clear conscience.

Dr. C. Oscar Johnson used to tell of training given Iroquois Indians who have built many of the steel frames for America's vast skyscrapers. They have a universal instruction given to each worker. It is, "Never lean against the wind." If the wind suddenly stops or changes directions, the tilting of the body will cause it to fall rapidly to the ground. Therefore, their motto is "Never lean against the wind," regardless of its pressure. It is good advice for steel workers and for administrators.

# 8
# From Where I Sat

By its very nature, the Sunday School Board exists at the eye of a storm. It never knows much relief from troubled times and has experienced crisis after crisis throughout its lifetime.

Historically, the Sunday School Board came into existence at the suggestion of I. T. Tichenor, corresponding secretary of the Home Mission Board. He discovered through experience that an institution which promotes missions cannot publish educational materials at the same time.

Perhaps there has never been a more brilliant leader among Southern Baptists than Dr. Tichenor. He observed that the more successful he was in publishing, the more apt the churches were to get angry and reduce their contributions to his missionary enterprises. He suggested a publishing house to serve as a lightning rod to pull away the static electricity which his board was experiencing. He is the one who suggested such an institution to J. M. Frost. The Sunday School Board was brought into existence after years of heated debate before the Convention. It has been free of controversy for only brief periods of time throughout its existence.

If an executive secretary-treasurer, or president as the title now stands, were not aware of this fact, he would tend to wonder what he was doing that was so wrong. The letters of every chief executive's office in the history of the institution read almost identically. One can go back into the files and update the letters that have been there for decades, and they read just like today's letters dealing with the same subjects. The lingering problems are essentially the same. This means controversy of some type is unavoidable almost continuously in the institution. Every leader of the operation must be emotionally equipped for it.

Many factors contribute to this situation. One is that the Sunday School Board has to deal with theological interpretation. Theological concepts have many variations in the Southern Baptist Convention. It would be impossible for the Convention to function as a democracy without such variations, but this means that every time a person says something in print it will not be exactly according to the thoughts of some reader. A letter is usually shot back in rebuttal.

Many letters of criticism may not be related to the president, but he gets them just the same. He is held responsible for them so he must deal with them.

When I arrived in Nashville in 1953, there was a stack of letters on my desk from people I had never known. They had heard I was elected and they were seeing to it that their words were filed with me in my early days, so they had written before my arrival.

One of the letters was from a man who was exceedingly brilliant intellectually but evidently had no sensitivity about the feelings of others. He had lots of sense but little judgment. Anyway he decided he wanted to be head of one of the departments at the Sunday School Board. So the letter from him on my desk on arrival was not an appeal that he be chosen, but an ultimatum. He would do everything within his power to create problems for me if not elected. Of course he was not. Another letter was from a man who accused me of misappropriating Cooperative Program money. I wrote him that the Sunday School Board does not receive Cooperative Program gifts. I asked him how I could misappropriate money I had never received. His reply was that I was bound to be guilty because I ran around with that bunch who did handle such funds. In his last paragraph he switched his typewriter over to a red ribbon and with capital letters ended his correspondence with the sentence, "IT IS A SIN TO GIVE THROUGH THE COOPERATIVE PROGRAM." I wrote again, challenging this man on his own grounds. I knew he got a monthly check from a denominational agency, a part of which was Cooperative Program money. I said to him that if it is a sin to give to the Cooperative Program that it is also a sin to receive from it. I added that I would accept his words as truth when he returned the checks he had received. It was my last letter from him.

While some letters of this type are written because someone misunderstands or has only partial information, we get many simply because we are located several hundred miles away. We have understood this and have taken many of the letters in stride, knowing that the content has very little if anything to do with the reason for the letter. The writer just had to unload on somebody.

We had a letter from one church enclosing a church bulletin in which they were making severe printed attacks against us. The letter itself was apologizing, stating that their church was about to split. It seemed the only way they could unite their people was to turn them against us because we were several hundred miles away. They were diverting attention from their internal arguments trying to unify the people against us. As soon as the controversy had quieted a bit then the pastor assured us he would give us opportunity to visit there and try to recoup our resultant bad public relations with the people. While the article in the bulletin was severe in its condemnation, the accompanying letter was apologetic. Such a tactic was not rare in our experience. It does mean if we did not understand the background and deal with the problem philosophically rather than personally, we might develop emotional problems of our own.

While there were many letters of criticism about many subjects, and somebody somewhere seems to be against any step we take regardless of direction or nature, there have been only a few times in all these years when the situation developed into what could be considered a controversy. We refer to an episode as a milder type controversy. It does not run as deeply or last as long. Too, it is often built on emotion more than on a situation. Yet it is very real while it exists. Let me refer to two instances which I call episodes. They are the Baldwin episode and the *Becoming* episode. Also, I will describe the Elliot controversy and the controversy regarding Volume I of *The Broadman Bible Commentary* from the way they appeared to me where I sat.

The Baldwin episode was not unexpected. We knew the Supreme Court decision in 1954 was going to bring tremendous social upheaval the entire nation over and create immediate tensions in churches throughout the nation. Drastic changes of a revolutionary nature like that cannot be made instantaneously without corresponding emotional upheavals. Such would be disconcerting in the Convention. It could be catastrophic in some of the churches.

The Sunday School Board has always stressed the importance of human personality, the worth of persons, the equality of mankind before God. We had championed the idea of the Bible that nationality and racial extraction make no difference to the eyes of God. The song "Red, and yellow, black and white, they are precious in his sight" was taught to nearly every child in most every church. But in 1954 some of the churches began to feel that they were being coerced by government and law in matters related to their internal church operations. Because of the tradition of separation of church and state for which Baptists had contended since the Constitution's first amendment, written largely on Baptist insistence, the feelings were intensified. Already they were feeling there must be an easier and better way to correct a national wrong than by violent or military means to which government seemed to be resorting.

While Christians would have to agree with the ultimate objective, there were conscientious disagreements as to method used to bring such to pass.

The Sunday School Board was thrown into the dilemma of charting its course so as to help the churches maintain balance and make judgments that were right and lasting, that they would not regret later. So we followed a pattern by which we hoped transition could come without violent revolutions in the churches. Such could create irreparable breaches in fellowship.

Very few of the thirty-four thousand churches among Southern Baptists had any constitutional limitations of membership. This meant that officially they were not segregated. In fact, many of them practiced some degree of integration already. But in many areas only white prospects were visited by churches during enlistment times and invitations were extended only to the white people of the area to come to Sunday School and to unite with the church. Such a practice was followed by many churches out of courtesy to strong black conventions which insisted that our churches not practice "sheep stealing" among their members.

Because the Sunday School Board did not announce avowed opposition to the government's position and did not openly attack integration on moral and scriptural grounds, there were extremists who organized against us to try to force us into the position of arguing in our printed materials that God made us different and therefore wanted us to be kept separate.

There are evidences that at least three extremist organizations, the Ku Klux Klan, John Birch Society, and White Citizens Council, were looking for grounds of major attack against the Sunday School Board. They were found in a youth publication for Training Union for July 4, 1964, where a bibliography listed the title of a book written by a black author named Baldwin. In the lesson procedure it was listed with other titles with a statement inviting Training Union group members who might have read any of these books to share with other members their impressions of problems of Negroes.

The writer of this particular part of the lesson procedure was one of our employees. He had not read the book by Baldwin but listed it on the suggestion of someone else, intending for it to be checked out before publication. Procedures required such.

It is understandable that many people reacted adversely to the listing of this title even though it was not recommended and there were no quotes from the book given. The title was just listed in a bibliography. Unfortunately, when the manuscript crossed the desk of the editor of that publication where procedures called for the editor to check any book list personally, it was at a time when the editor had just resigned. Four people were serving in different capacities on that particular issue. So there was not an editor as such at that moment to check book lists. The title got into print unawares in that way.

The people who were looking for some particular point to attack us found it here. The issue flared at the time the November presidential election was underway, and the extremists were trying to coerce us to handle their purely political materials in Baptist Book Stores. We refused. This political angle only added fuel to the fire and produced underground attack against the denomination in general and the Sunday School Board in particular.

Perhaps the most damaging aspect came from some person or

organization called "The Circuit Riders." They took pages filled with
filthy words from the Baldwin book. After photostating our Training
Union cover jackets, they inserted in printed form on the other side
this vulgar content in such a way as to leave the impression that
this had been printed in the Training Union quarterly. You could
imagine the upset when such false propaganda was mailed to masses
of churches. Some of the most sincere Baptists, seeing the false propaganda, wondered what was happening to Southern Baptists. No book
store had stocked the book, and no church had used it. We had seen
to that.

Exactly opposite the Baldwin episode was the *Becoming* episode.
This was another publication which brought anger to the social activists. They had attempted to force us to an outright aggressive
integration stance in the churches. It is interesting that their techniques
were almost identical to the segregation extremists. Their attacks were
just as vicious and unjust.

The *Becoming* episode flared when, as editor-in chief of all publications, I had requested that a section of this publication for fourteen-
year-old pupils be pulled in order that three corrections could be
made before mailing. Under our quality-control system, we reserve
the right up to the time of filing a copy of any publication with
the post office—at which instant it legally becomes a publication—to
make corrections in any of the 125 magazine-type publications we
produce. Once there has been post office distribution, however,
changes can be made by the elected Board only.

The *Becoming* episode grew out of a question raised by our art
department concerning a picture they had selected and had planned
to use of one black man and two white girl college students in
conference in a college library. First, the picture had used college-age
students, when guidelines called for pictures of fourteen- or fifteen-
year-old youths for whom the publication was being produced. Then
the process through which they had put the picture exaggerated that
difference in age and raised other visual problems also. The fact that
both races appeared in the same picture was what got the national
publicity, even though this had happened hundreds of times before
in our publications without difficulty. That was not it.

There was also a paragraph in the quarterly dealing with the sensitivity problem with which we had been struggling. This had nothing to do with race, but was acute at the time. There was yet another problem in the approach of the teacher's quarterly at the same lesson. It tended to coerce the churches, confronting them on critical social issues without previous notification or preparation. Therefore, we asked that the entire section be pulled and revisions made at three places. We gave authorization for the same lesson on the same subject to be run in a subsequent edition. My personal suggestion was that the picture used should show fourteen and fifteen-year-old black and white boys and girls seated around a table. Such would be far more understandable and would fit into the nature of the lesson written.

News reports of the incident were evidently initiated by a former Nashvillian living in New York. He seemed to be unfriendly toward institutions because of his personal experience while serving as associate editor of a far-out journal, not Baptist, that had come under attack by its constituency and was abolished.

To complicate the situation, press reports across the country carried distortions of the true situation. A local Nashville newspaper kept the matter in headlines far beyond its actual news value, and wire services repeated misstatements nationwide. Never is it possible to correct such erroneous reports. We do not have access to the names of all the publications which printed incorrect information, and attempts at correction are usually separated such a long time from the original story and run in such inconspicuous places that readers of the original seldom see the corrected facts.

I have evidence satisfactory to my own mind that not only did one local newspaper writer make this a matter of personal crusade, but that the interests of one of the publishing houses producing material for black churches were involved.

This publishing house, privately owned, issued a public statement condemning our administrative action. The statement did not reveal that the same publisher had been using our manuscripts in their publications for decades. Nor did it reveal that their own interests would be best served at this time by a resegregation psychology which would have resulted in greater use by black churches of their literature rather than ours.

The Sunday School Board came through both of these episodes unscathed, although battered mercilessly for months. Still the Sunday School Board's volume of business continued to expand, so the purposes of the critics were not accomplished.

The Elliott controversy was quite another matter. It dealt with our publication of a book by Broadman Press with the title *The Message of Genesis* by Ralph Elliott. He was professor at Midwestern Baptist Theological Seminary, Kansas City.

The book was prepared basically for teaching purposes and was written by one of the most evangelistic professors in the entire Southern Baptist seminary system. The author, an able pulpiteer, was considered by the religious world to be basically a conservative theologian. Some of the content of the book, however, was to many of the readers new and a bit foreign, so controversy arose which ultimately resulted in the resignation of Dr. Elliott from the seminary faculty. Vigorous attacks against Broadman Press and the Sunday School Board were unleashed in consecutive Convention sessions in San Francisco and Kansas.

When the book was being produced, our inside procedure called for a committee to evaluate manuscripts and present recommendations to the administrative staff. This was done. The committee studying this manuscript stated that it had difficulty formulating a recommendation. Publication could result in controversy in the Convention. So the committee deemed it unwise to publish the manuscript at that time.

The dilemma we faced was that the recommendation of the Convention's Survey Committee (Branch Committee) were in full implementation at the time. The committee, sustained by the Convention, maintained that the Sunday School Board should produce for other agencies the published works they needed in the furtherance of their assignments. This fixed us with responsibility without control of content.

Under Baptist polity one agency cannot make decisions about internal operations of another agency. If we sought to force revision of the book at the Sunday School Board we would have been tampering with curriculum material for a theological school. If we refused to publish the book desired by another agency we would be violating a Convention directive. Our only other option was to produce the manuscript submitted. All three options were dead-end streets. We knew we were in difficulty any way we went.

After much discussion we decided administratively that we should publish the manuscript as it was. We sought to establish the fact that it was a book prepared for teaching purposes. It was being produced by the Sunday School Board under the Broadman Press imprint, not for use in Sunday Schools. There appeared printed attacks that this book was being produced for Sunday School lesson course materials, else it would not have been produced by the Sunday School Board. So misunderstanding abounded. Personal and institutional consequences were many and severe.

The controversy concerning Volume I of *The Broadman Bible Commentary* was even more complex in nature and was due in part to a basic misunderstanding. Many thought we were producing the commentary the Southern Baptist Convention had requested in its 1965 Dallas meeting about which there were specific stipulations given. They confused the requested one-volume commentary with the twelve-volume one which had been in process a number of years even before that 1965 request had been made. *The Broadman Bible Commentary* was being produced for serious students of the Scripture who wanted a depth approach based more directly on the original languages.

Actually there was a sizable group among Southern Baptists who were opposed to our producing a commentary of any kind. Conversely, we felt that the Southern Baptist Convention had reached a stage of development and maturity sufficient for successful production of more scholarly volumes for Southern Baptists who wanted such. We felt our Baptist people ought to be aware of what was being said and done by scholars in the theological world whether they agreed or not. They should make up their minds in the light of their own experiences and personal interpretations regardless of any position a commentary might take in its treatment of any passage.

Some were attacking content of the commentary even before the writers had been chosen. This revealed the heated opposition some had for a commentary of any kind. It was our feeling that Dr. Clifton J. Allen, longtime editorial secretary and onetime secretary of the Editorial Division, was the only man we had with enough experience and technical skill to be general editor of a series like the planned *Broadman Bible Commentary* which our trustees had authorized. Therefore our appeal was that he take this as a major assignment and the crowning work of his long tenure at the Board in the editorial field. Even though there is no such thing as a perfect printed work, I think history will prove this the greatest work of Dr. Allen's editorial career. Constant streams of compliments from readers verify the fact that a superb job was done by him in the process.

One of the problems inherent in producing a commentary is that every verse of Scripture has to be dealt with. This is quite different from sermon preparation, where a pastor can choose one text or pass over another without being forced to harmonize the two in the same sermon. The pulpit, therefore, does not have to deal with the same kind of problem an editor of a commentary does. The problem of harmonizing all Scripture passages requires tedious analysis, depth of insight, and tremendous skills. It was our feeling that Dr. Allen, with writers whom he would recommend for the various volumes, and consulting editors, could produce just that sort of needed series.

Rather than label *The Broadman Bible Commentary* a conservative, moderate, or progressive publication, it was decided that we would not label it at all. We did write its nature and objectives in detail and had them approved by the trustees. The same was true of the methods and timetable to be followed and a number of other guidelines that would govern its production.

For instance, it was agreed that writers needed to express several theological views where there was diversity of opinion. There was also the requirement that in discussing different opinions the writer would be thoroughly objective without appearing condescending toward any who might disagree. We also stated that where several viewpoints generally were held, after objective discussion the writer could insert his own personal view at that point if he wished, if he followed the above directive.

Most of *The Broadman Bible Commentary* has been accepted enthusiastically and without difficulty. It is understandable that Volume I would be the issue that would face the greatest number of hazards because of the nature and difficulties of the Hebrew language, because a previous controversy had raged over a previous book dealing with the same chapters of Genesis, and because theories of inspiration were dealt with in an introductory article. The latter is another highly emotional topic.

After considering a number of potential writers for the manuscript on the first part of Volume I, it was decided that Dr. G. Henton Davies of England, one of the noted scholars of the Baptist Union of Great Britain and Ireland, would be an appropriate person to invite, since we hoped the volume would have international usage. He accepted the invitation when it was extended and proceeded with his work, submitting portions to Dr. Allen for review and analysis in the course of development. It was surprising that when controversy flared it centered around Davies' treatment of Abraham's offering of Isaac.

Few readers (if, indeed, some critics actually read the volume), ever realized that he was actually dealing with the question of the consistency of God, seeking to harmonize this incident with such verses in the New Testament which say "God tempts no man." At first glance the two Scripture passages seem to say opposite things about God. The question immediately issues, "Is he the same God with the same nature and commandments in both the Old Testament and the New?" It is a basic unavoidable question, even if it is one of faith and not doubt.

Dr. Davies stated that Abraham's offering of Isaac was a real historical incident. At no place does he question the historicity of the experience. In trying to emphasize that this was an incident which God permitted rather than decreed—which would be an allowable interpretation by the very nature of the Hebrew language—he termed Abraham's own impression that God must have directly ordered it as "the climax of the psychology of his life." Therefore, certain critics concluded that Davies was saying that this was not a historical incident but something that merely went on in the mind of Abraham. Too,

Dr. Davies used the words *"our* answer" referring editorially to his own interpretation. Those who opposed claimed he was attempting to use the "our" in reference to a Southern Baptist position. They did not want to be positionized in that way.

Such problems would have been complex enough within themselves. To add to the complexity, Volume I unfortunately got mixed up with the Atlanta conference of the Christian Life Commission which was under vicious attack at the same time. The Commission had invited a *Playboy* magazine official and a "situation ethics" professor to have a confrontation with them in Atlanta. Some of the extreme rightist organizations felt that the Christian Life Commission, by giving these persons a platform, was actually recommending them. The press gave much coverage to the Atlanta Conference, preceding the Denver Southern Baptist Convention. In news releases in our Baptist papers and elsewhere the last paragraph, after dealing in detail with the Atlanta Conference, would often end with some such suggestion as "the other controversial issue to be dealt with in Denver was Volume I of *The Broadman Bible Commentary.*"

Unfortunately some of the readers identified Volume I with the Christian Life Commission and the Atlanta Conference when there was no relationship. Therefore it was hopelessly enmeshed in the emotional spillover, and we began to wonder, two or three weeks before Denver, whether Volume I could survive so much misunderstanding and emotion.

While many sincere conscientious people opposed the commentary at Denver, there were others engaging in attacks who evidently had personal motives and motivations. Some were trying to start extremist publications and were testing the Denver audience for purposes of predicting possible circulation. Others were trying to start independent Bible schools or seminaries and were seeking to publicize their own doctrinal positions so messengers could know the theological stance their school would take. Others had still other reasons, many personal, others more objective. Altogether the opposition was too much.

The result was that the Convention requested that Volume I be rewritten. The trustees of the Sunday School Board could never be quite sure just what the Convention meant. Their understanding of what the Convention intended to say and what it actually said were not in harmony.

Technically, before one can "rewrite" a commentary he had to have written the book in the first place. Just as a person cannot review a lesson he has not viewed, so an author cannot rewrite a book he has not written. So the way the motion was stated seemed to imply that Davies himself had to do the rewriting. This was required if the motion of the Convention was to be carried out literally.

Davies was coming to the United States for an extended speaking tour. At that time as president of the Baptist Union in Ireland he would have been scheduled to speak at the Southern Baptist Convention in St. Louis, which courtesy had been extended presidents of the Baptist Union of Great Britain and Ireland for many years. He graciously declined to come because of the controversy over his writings. It was the request of our trustees that we would have an interview with Davies after his arrival in America. Then we would chart our course from there. Both he and we were anxious for a discussion to see just where the real problems were. Davies had assured us that he would do everything within his power to produce the type volume Southern Baptists wanted. Furthermore, he stated that if he could not conscientiously do what the Convention wanted he would eliminate himself from the project totally. Then we could proceed to get any writer we wished and start anew. Our trustees felt opportunity should first be given to Davies to redo his work to make it acceptable to Southern Baptists if that were possible.

Added to the already delicate situation was the fact that Davies, the author whose work had been rejected, was president of a sister Baptist convention in the Baptist World Alliance. Thus we were dealing not with just a man, or a man and a book. Rather, we were dealing in inter-convention relationships between the Southern Baptist Convention and the Baptist Union of Great Britain and Ireland in the entire matter. It is unfortunate that some who did not understand the delicacy of such a situation felt that we were either dragging our feet intentionally or resisting the Convention's actions altogether. Instead, we were trying to keep all bases covered so that when things were once settled there would not be lasting scars remaining between

Baptist bodies internationally.

Unfortunately when we came to the Convention the following year in St. Louis, we had not been able to have the scheduled conferences with Davies. These meetings had been scheduled for immediately after that Convention. Some of the more impatient brethren there renewed their attack on the Sunday School Board, implying that we had not done anything about the matter, although we had spent thousands of man-hours on it. They insisted on immediate action.

The Sunday School Board has weathered these attacks with an amazing degree of resilience. It attests to the institution's health and says that the Southern Baptist Convention is gaining in maturity and strength along with size. It validates the claim that we as Baptists are able to deal with problems and come through them without permanent scars, even though the issues seem terribly acute at the moment.

Something that helps make the handling of controversies more tolerable are the funny incidents that occur. They give us laughter even in the tensest moments of difficulty. There was not much funny about the controversy related to Volume I or the Elliott matter, but in other areas many laughs have occurred and with frequency. Look at a few.

We had produced a wonderful Sex Education Series. It had been highly acceptable among Southern Baptists because of its Christian context and terminology. In fact, it has met a real need especially for parents and youth workers.

A certain man had ordered a book on sex education. Since all materials in our warehouse are coded by number the punchcard operator handling the order punched the code for the shipping room. The girl at the punchcard machine in error pushed the wrong button and gave the wrong code number to the warehouse concerning this man's order. The thing of such humor was that he had ordered a book on sex education. The title sent him was our new Broadman book *Too Old to Learn*.

We have had a number of other funny incidents to occur. Some have come through typographical errors such as the sermon subject where the preacher was writing on "Why I Believe in Immortality."

The typesetter had come out with "Why I Believe in Immorality." The type was on the presses when the error was discovered.

Letters that have come to the Sunday School Board have provided much laughter because of wording, content, or misunderstanding of the institution's purposes and mission. Smiles and chuckles have helped balance the tensions produced by controversies. One of the things that has helped us endure the pressure has been that sweets have been mixed with the bitters, so in the overall it has been bearable.

Some of the letters have been so brief and to the point that we haven't known just how to handle them. Such was a letter saying: "Please tell me what the Bible teaches. Limit comments to half a page." Another we never quite fathomed. It read: "Please send me the Sunday School Board without obligation. Sincerely yours." Then there were those letters in which someone had heard orally a title of some famous book, but misunderstood, and still tried to order one. One such incident was when a lady had heard about Dale Evans' excellent book, *Angel Unaware.* She ordered *Some Angels' Underwear.* Even more laughable was the letter of a lady who ordered *A Fat Man Speaks.* We had never produced a book by that title. Likely we would have never figured out what she had in mind had not the intuition of one of the women clerks in a Baptist Book Store assisted us. It dawned on her that what the lady wanted was *Broadman Comments.*

One of the deep mysteries is how the psychology of the '70's is in such utter contrast to the psychology of the 60's. Earlier we had discussed the rebellion of the 60's which every institution of influence experienced. All were under attack simultaneously.

The 70's have been just the opposite. We have received as many compliments since the turn of the decade as we have criticisms. The amazing thing is how many people have written apologies for earlier letters they had typed in anger and without having facts in hand. Later when they learned the true situation they were fair enough to drop a note of apology for their earlier precipitous action.

# 9
# On Our Way Up

The chapters presented thus far have looked backward to events already transpired. This last chapter looks forward to what I feel is ahead for the Board and Southern Baptists. The forward glance demands a backward look since the past is prologue to the future.

On the previous pages I have tried to describe my impressions and give my understandings of things after more than two decades of experience in a very sensitive position in the denomination's life. In some ways the position has been related, directly or indirectly, to every denominational tempest. It is where stabilization must take place during crucial times, or results can be detrimental if not catastrophic.

From where I sat I got the peculiar perspectives of the factors and persons involved in given situations. I have tried to list in the discussions those matters which are usually not recorded in minutes of the meetings, but have had to do more with the subjects under discussion in the corridors or private conversation.

The headaches of these years have been tremendous. At times the load was almost beyond physical endurance because so many important things which demanded attention would be happening simultaneously. We have had to establish priorities in the light of the overall welfare, not the individual demands. At times we have had to hold off decisions in certain areas although they were considered urgent by certain people. Solutions could not come then until problems elsewhere had been solved first.

Things had to come in systematic sequence. It has been much like playing checkers where a dozen moves must be made before one could get at the "man" he is to capture next. Unless one understands the science of checkers, he cannot see the necessity of this principle in day-to-day administration.

There is another sense in which the administrator is like a judge in a courtroom, although he cannot always be as deliberate in his decisions. Time will not allow. He cannot call in every witness related to each problem arising. Decisions have to be made too quickly in administration for such detailed attention to be allowed. Nevertheless, the administrator has to evaluate circumstances, call in some of the persons related to get their best judgments, put it all together in his own system of prayerful analysis, and act. At other times on the spur of the moment he must decide without having benefit of consultation of any kind because a deadline for a publication has arrived. He can only pray that he has gotten enough facts together to make his decisions correct.

Not only must there be the understanding of circumstances, there must also be the understanding of people. Frequently problems relate to people who do not even understand themselves. Nevertheless they have voices and votes in a convention and can create tremendous problems for any administrative officer if they go unnoted. Certain people are apt to operate either on a hunch or a prejudice, or build their actions on the foundation of some former unfortunately produced hostility which has accelerated their emotions. Occasionally there is a person who hits a convention floor because it is the only place he can get the public attention he feels he deserves. All too often this is due to his own disposition or that of the woman he married who might dominate his home or church, and who does not allow him full expression in his local situations. Those of us who have lived in sensitive situations through many years must exercise patience and judgment here and try to determine whether a person has a legitimate complaint, or whether he really is giving vent to pent-up emotions from an entirely different source which he can no longer contain.

It is amazing how many times the person who makes a motion or introduces a resolution or leads a crusading action on the convention floor is not the ringleader in the movement which he is vocalizing. Many times he becomes the voice of someone else who remains unidentified. Because of this it is very difficult to know the nature of your opposition until you can first discover who the real spokesman is. Then, and only then you can begin your analysis in the light of that understanding.

One of the problems which has plagued me most has been the speed with which certain organizations, pastors' conferences, and the like are willing to wire "resolutions of condemnation" and give wide publicity thereto without even inquiring about the facts of the case. I have in mind a telegram from a certain pastors' conference in one of our strongest Baptist cities demanding the immediate termination of William J. Reynolds, who now heads our Church Music Department. Oddly enough the demand was stated on the basis of a rumor that he no longer believed in heaven. Such was ridiculously false, but the wire came nevertheless. A letter apparently seemed too slow.

All Dr. Reynolds had done was to express to a newspaper reporter the wish that preachers would preach about heaven oftener so that congregations could sing about it more. Then a careless reporter in a display of slovenly writing, after he had quoted the above comment, began to editorialize on why preachers don't preach about heaven oftener. Religious News Service unfortunately misread the reporter's article and issued a nationwide press release identifying Reynolds as a famous Southern Baptist song leader who did not believe in heaven. This was exactly opposite from what had been said. Of course, I would have been most foolish to have disciplined Dr. Reynolds on such a ridiculous and unjustified demand, so I did nothing.

As we face the future, it is my hope that we can manifest more maturity now that our Convention is coming of age in years and size. Some things that have "rocked the boat" in the past should not be experienced by my successor in office.

One of the more difficult things to face is extremism. There is a certain degree of tolerance beyond which an institution cannot go. The moment an administrative officer begins to level off the swing of an institution and say that we can go no further in a certain direction, he brings upon himself the hostilities of passionate extremists who feel that they are in the middle of the road and everybody else is an extremist. Actually these critics are so often on the fringe of the whole denominational structure and are unaware of it.

Fundamentalism with a capital *F* has always been a problem in

Southern Baptist life even though most all of us are fundamentalists with a little *f.* We are justifiably proud of that position. Actually, there are few "modernists" in any Southern Baptist life. If anyone seems so inclined, he usually eliminates himself before he becomes a problem to the denomination. A modernist will not fit in the solidly conservative climate of Southern Baptist Convention life. He would find himself very unhappy and ineffective. Fear of modernism in the Southern Baptist Convention is a false fear. Usually such is drummed up by certain people who are trying to foster an extremism at the other end of the line. Some have even sought to establish a legalism akin to Pharisaism. It is good they have failed.

It is not the theological position of Fundamentalism which is hurtful. It is the pharisaical spirit. Legalism is as deadly as modernism and should be resisted to the same degree. Many times those holding extremely Fundamentistic positions have emotional problems of their own. Sometimes they are spiritual problems of a deep nature. In fleeing modernism we cannot run into the fold of crass Fundamentalism. In fleeing Fundamentalism we cannot run into modernism. We must take a solid middle, conservative stance. There we will stand fast because there our people are. We must do this unapologetically.

Racism will continue to be a problem in some churches. It has never really been a problem in others. In fact there are churches in the Southern Baptist Convention which have had Negroes in membership through their entire history, some for more than a hundred years. Very few churches have constitutional limitations on membership as regards race. This means that most churches can deal with a situation when it arises and do what seems to be best in regard to it at the time. Many of our churches are ready for integration now. Some are not. Each church must determine its own readiness. Churches must enter into these individual decisions unhurriedly and without coercion. If they can make choices deliberately and objectively, they can be lasting. Where fellowships are free and friendships open, a church has no serious problems. Christ gives answers.

Fellowship is one of the basic characteristics of a church. Membership, therefore, should never be forced, but always relaxed and free. The church that has problems with a closed racial membership needs to go through a process of vigorous self-examination and education to discover Christ's concept of humanity. A Christian attitude must be maintained toward all men. When the tensions are gone and threats removed, the problem seems to find a practical, happy solution.

The millennial question is a tedious one that some people try to make a basis of fellowship also. They seek to stand firm and adamantly condemn others who do not see things exactly as they do with reference to the second coming of Christ. Even though in basic belief I am a premillennialist, I would vigorously oppose the Southern Baptist Convention's taking a strong premillennialist stand. It is our job to be prepared for Christ's coming and to help others get prepared for that inevitable hour. Beyond that point everything else is God's decision anyway. Why should we busy ourselves trying to handle God's business or work out God's schedule? Why should we seek to know what he has not seen fit to reveal even to the angels? The millennial question, therefore, ought to be one that is left open so premillennial, postmillennial, or amillennial views can be held by brethren who respect each other even though their opinions might be diametrically opposed.

More acute just now is the problem of Pentecostalism. Really it is sort of neopentecostalism which has appeared in some form in many denominations in the last decade. It is misunderstood by some people and feared by others. Even Pentecostal preachers have expressed their concern that this present tendency has reached an extreme position in America and is producing too much emotionalism and introversion. They lament that the people are not addressing themselves enough to the problems of this world in the here and now. When this happens the movement can become an escape mechanism rather than a spiritual blessing.

Of course, our Baptist position has always been to recognize the power of the Holy Spirit and submit to his guidance. The key is to use many Scripture passages to measure whether the Holy Spirit has actually filled a life, or whether that person has had some emotional experience quite different from those of early Christians. One may misunderstand his own emotional experience. He can end up with a sense of pride, causing him to look down on everyone else. Therefore he can feel superior because he feels he has been blessed of God in a unique way.

The sense of pride is deadly within itself. Too, it is so contrary to New Testament teachings. Anyone filled with the Holy Spirit is also filled with a spirit of humility. Any time a person brags unduly or condescendingly about his experience of personal spiritual infilling is making a confession that his is not really a deep spiritually infilling. Rather, it is some misunderstood emotional extremism which he has totally misread. One can be filled with a spirit, or with spirits, other than the Holy Spirit.

While some churches have been torn asunder because neopentecostalism in the membership has gotten out of hand, the rank and file of our Southern Baptist churches have taken the movement in stride. Where it has hit a church unexpectedly, that church may have been shocked. Most have been patient and understanding. Some churches have doubled their assignments to these people who have expressed their sincerity and desire to serve. They have been given visitation tasks which are very important in the community, such as hospital services or rescue mission work. This is a wonderful way to deal with a problem like the Pentecostal movement. The Southern Baptist Convention is faced with this problem to a degree but should not be fearful because it has appeared on the horizon. This is the third wave I have seen in my years in the ministry. Therefore I have not felt threatened by it. I have seen such situations come and phase out before. Some churches have been helped by the experience. They have given guidance to the people and have led them in studying the Scriptures more seriously. A quest for the Holy Spirit's enlightenment as well as his power should be one of our prayers.

Some Southern Baptists have feared the status quo more than the neopentecostal movement. Some churches do not want changes of any kind at any time. They resist all efforts at revision or improvement, even revival. Churches like this are gradually phasing out because a church must expand if it is to thrive or even survive spiritually or numerically. Churches which try to hold their own rather than expand to win a world will go through an aging process in which the majority of the church leaders ultimately become older adults. Such only adds to the already existing conservativism of the church body. It means that the church can no longer be vigorous and outreaching in its efforts. Such a church tends to become increasingly inactive even though its members may be much more able monetarily to finance a church program than some young aggressive membership with a large number of children involved.

As the Southern Baptist Convention grows older, this is one of the practical problems it too must face. It ought to meet this tendency toward the status quo with planned solutions to overcome them. Churches and the Convention can be kept young and vigorous. They must maintain an outreach program and ministry of missions. They can deal with and master living situations although they may be difficult.

As we face the future and its problems, we should resist the status quo and call for creativity as well as sacrificial commitment.

One of the problems we must solve in our denomination is the mode of operation of the Convention itself. Problems now exist because of our size which were not experienced when the Convention was young and small. The larger a body becomes the more complex its operations get. Solutions are not easy. Discussions must be more deliberate. Lasting solutions must be sought. Some of the more aggravating and perplexing problems never get on the Convention floor for discussion. Somehow the Convention tends to refer these to committees. Such referrals, if resorted to too often, tend to reduce the Convention's status as a deliberative body. If the present trend continues the annual Convention sessions will become largely inspirational meetings with sermons, live drama, and plenty of action but little business except abbreviated reports. The question must be asked, Is this best?

Basic in our denomination's nature is the necessity for discussion of vital issues and the giving of clear directions. If this is not done by the annual body of the Convention in full session after ample discussion, solutions will be neither sound nor accepted. They will be far from lasting. The problems of bigness can sometimes be more acute than the problems of littleness. This needs to be understood too. Our people must deliberately plan for the business sessions of the Convention and defend the time for adequate discussion. If we fail here we can gravitate unconsciously into a Presbyterian system of denominational administration and lose our Baptist character. The question which must be asked is, Will Baptist churches accept this change in Baptist polity, even if they themselves have allowed it to come to pass?

My closeness to the denomination in these years has made me a more ardent Baptist than I have ever been. I appreciate the processes our forefathers developed. I hope we can maintain the autonomy of the local churches in fullest measure so they can be aggressive and dynamic. At the same time we must work together and find bases for closer cooperation and teamwork if we are to fulfil our responsible role as the largest evangelical body of North America. With our growth has come responsibility. For this reason we have an obligation to develop a program and provide materials and programs to do a better job. It is a stewardship we must keep if we are faithful to God and our Baptist forebears.

One of the things the Southern Baptist Convention inevitably faces because of size is its tendency toward fragmentation. This has been the experience of all large religious groups. While we are doing everything humanly possible to keep this from occurring, it is a growing danger as long as the Convention continues to enlarge. And it should and will get larger. If we understand what is happening and know how to safeguard against it, we can preserve all the liberties of the individuals and the churches and still work together within the framework of a highly organized denominational structure. We can experience massive spiritual achievements over the world which could never be achieved by any one church, state convention, or section of our denomination. It is of utmost importance, therefore, that we find ways of close cooperation which will be most meaningful and even deepening in spirit as the years pass.

Another problem we face is getting a broader participation and involvement of Baptist personnel in the development of church programs on a long-range basis. A program will be like a strange language to many people unless they can have participation in the early planning processes. Just how to do this in a denomination like ours is the basic question. Long-range planning is imperative in Southern Baptist Convention life. Involvement in planning processes should be as broad as reason will allow. Understandably everyone or every area cannot participate in such a process. Nevertheless, every segment of the denomination can be represented by someone who can verbalize the concepts of a particular group to make sure that their wishes are at least considered as future directions are charted and developed.

One of the human problems we face after group planning is done is that suggestions and ideas can be received and worked into a program, but these are not identifiable once that program has reached its final stage. It is not too different from the baking of a cake calling for sugar, lard, flour, spices, and many other things. All of these are necessary ingredients, each contributing to the overall quality. When the cake is a finished product, however, none of these individual ingredients is identifiable. One who has contributed the lard is apt to say, "I don't see my ingredient." The ones who added sugar can say the same. So can the ones who added spices, flour, and the other ingredients. Each can comment likewise and be correct. In meshing ingredients each loses its identity. Therefore a person cannot follow to completion his own contribution to a product. This frustrates some people and they conclude that their suggestions have been ignored by the planning group. Such is the case even though their ideas may have been implemented fully into the planning process. Much like the bloodstream, it has filtered through the entire human body. Still, because of this invisible principle all participants cannot identify their individual contributions. Sometimes they blame big denominations for planning without consulting them when their ideas have been incorporated throughout but have lost their individual identities.

Another problem is that people are apt to say that denominational leaders sit at a desk and plan what those people "down" in the local churches are to do. This very statement reveals a misconception. Churches are not "down" in the Southern Baptist Convention. They are "up." All planning has to done with this in mind. Whether a church implements a program or not, and how far it goes into that implementation depends on that church's acceptance of an idea. Never

are denominational plans forced upon churches, yet it is very clear
that churches which cooperate with overall denominational plans are
the ones who are strongest and best in the long run. They have the
most dedicated membership and the most unselfish participation in
worldwide mission endeavors.

When all is said and done, all programs have to be on a broad
base if we are to serve to the very diverse situations in which we
as Southern Baptists find ourselves. This is understandable too. A
Convention like ours is made up of people who are very different.
They are not only operating in different situations, but frequently
their attitudes and evaluations are most diverse.

The most basic truth all Baptists must advocate is "Jesus is Lord."
We must seek to find his will fully and implement it completely in
every geographical location. In him we find our unity, our affection
each for the other. In him comes unity of purpose in all that we
do. This means that even though some churches may take different
routes to reach their objectives, as long as all are seeking to know
and do the will of God we will be moving together in the same general
areas of work doing things in ways that are not incompatible. The
end result will produce a greater fellowship among fellow believers
who love each other because Christ loves all. So Christ is magnified
and his will sought. Herein is our basis of unity and cooperation.

I cannot close this chapter which discusses our future without a
word concerning the man God has made available as my successor
as president of the Sunday School Board.

Never before in history has there been an installation service for
the chief executive officer of the Board. Evidently changes in administration have been too turbulent, and the incoming man has had as
his first duty the stilling of unsettled waters. Unfortunately, too many
people have aspired to the office, and some have sought the place
with aggressive, organized promotion. Never have any gotten the job
that way. The only thing they achieved was to create headaches for
themselves and the man who did get the job. Too often the organizations of the aspirants to the office have continued as pockets of
opposition to try to bog down the new administration. My early days
were hard enough, but would not compare with the experiences of

some of my predecessors.

Upon assuming office in 1953, I resolved that such difficulties should be forestalled, and that if I lived to retirement I would assume personal responsibility for effecting a smooth transition, maintaining continuity in operations to make it easier for my successor. I became convinced if this were to be accomplished my successor needed to be chosen one year before assuming his full weight of responsibilities. This I recommended, and the trustees concurred.

After working with the trustees just long enough to set up the system whereby they could work effectively and confidentially, I backed away, resolved to be unrelated totally to the process from that point on.

The first person who told me that Dr. Grady Cothen, president of the New Orleans Baptist Theological Seminary, was the one chosen for nomination by the committee was Dr. Cothen himself. I did know enough about the process to be convinced that cautious objective evaluation of every kind had been made so the selection could be accepted with confidence and conviction. A better choice could not have been made. He is God's man for this hour in this place. Support of Dr. Cothen's selection has been evidenced within the Board and throughout the Convention.

Since 1891, the Board has written glorious history. My forecast is that its greatest history is yet to be written, and that some of its brightest pages are now taking shape under the leadership of God.

Along with Simeon, I can rejoice in what my eyes are seeing before my departure from the scene.